GIDEON'S WAY

GIDEON'S WAY

GIDEON SCOTT MAY

Alloway Publishing

Alloway Publishing Ltd
Hastings Square Darvel
Ayrshire Scotland

First published in book form 1993

Copyright © Gideon Scott May

ISBN 0-907526-61-6

Designed and printed by Walker & Connell Ltd.
and The Cromwell Press

Fondly dedicated
to
Mum and Dad

Contents

The Homecoming

*As the first of the winter visitors arrive at Croft Douglas,
Gideon remembers a time when things weren't quite so
peaceful . . .*

Schiehallion, the hill of the fairies, is always the first to signal
the arrival of Tummelside's winter weather, by wearing a snow white
cape with a matching peaked cap to seemingly keep its head and
shoulders warm.

This also gives added protection from hard night frosts for the
birds and animals, like ptarmigan and hill hares, who would never
think of leaving their homes high in the mountains, even in the
wintertime.

This morning, the fairy mountain is sitting back admiring its
reflection in the clear, still, ice-cold water, possibly wondering
how soon it will be wearing a much longer white winter garment
which will reach all the way down to tentatively touch Loch
Tummel.

There's still another sign that winter is with us once again. An
outsize shadowy arrow is seen silhouetted against the sky as it flies
through the duck egg blue of the dawn, growing bigger and bigger.

It's a flock of wild geese from Greenland and Iceland coming
to spend at least the next five months with us.

It is such a comfort to see and hear them at this time of year
because these birds have, with an inbuilt instinct, chosen to come
and winter with us, believing our weather will be much warmer
than the land they have left so far behind.

Their leader, a great big gander, with a good deal of experience,
flies in front forming a tip to the arrow's Vee. When he gives the

signal "going down", with a strident honking call, the geese listen to their leader's command and prepare to land, following his instructions and actions implicitly.

Although wing weary after their long flight across the cream crested waves of the Norwegian Sea, the geese don't touch a bite until the leader warily looks around and swiftly selects sentinels to surround the flock before they're allowed to feed.

The chosen few are all ganders who are considered expendable, if necessary, but the geese have to be defended at all costs. Without them there would be no future flocks because they are the mothers and mothers-to-be.

The sentinels are big birds who are tired and hungry too, but will have to wait until they are relieved from duty. Besides keeping an ever vigilant watch over the feeding flock, the guards are prepared for a sudden approach by daring daylight predators and boldly meet any attack with stinging blows from their powerful wings.

The wild geese, although born swimmers with webbed feet, seem to spend most of their time on the land and will only rise and take to the water in an emergency, or at night when the foxes from the forests with their large families of grown-up cubs hunt together during the darkness.

Foxes don't like getting wet and, so they say, only go into water to get rid of fleas.

Among the geese I look especially for any who have been hatched and reared here and, no matter how far travelled, still call Croft Douglas home.

These were goslings or eggs, brought up by our broody hens after being abandoned by geese who had decided to nest here but were probably disturbed by predators.

The goslings, when they grow up, eventually answer the in-built call of the wild and go back with the rest to Iceland and Greenland.

It is always a heart-stopping moment when a goose leaves the flock that has just landed to instinctively seek the home it remembers so well. Tentatively, step by step, the wild goose walks towards me to take a piece of bread from my mouth, just as she used to do when only a little green and golden-yellow gosling.

Amongst my letters the other morning was an official-looking missive which said something like, "from information received we deem you a responsible person."

War-time experience taught me to be a trifle wary of the word "responsible" ever since being interviewed by a very senior officer regarding my future career in the RAF.

I was ushered into a deeply-carpeted room with huge oil paintings hanging on the walls and found myself facing the officer across a magnificent mahogany table.

He looked at me long and hard, then suddenly stood up and said, "Don't you think it's a bit stuffy in here, my lad? Let's go outside."

It was a beautiful, sunny, early summer day. The air was full of the fragrant smell of rhododendron flowers and vibrating with the buzzing of big bumble bees.

That was when the officer said, "I see by your records you are in your twenties. That means, old chap, you have now reached the age for promotion to a position of responsibility."

I wasn't long in finding out that this accolade actually meant more than just a probability of carrying the can for the mistakes and misdemeanours of others under your care or command.

I was eventually relieved of the responsibility by having to spend some considerable time in an RAF hospital.

It was a different world where kindly people cared for you.

Not that I enjoyed being confined to bed with my head bandaged but for the first time since volunteering to serve my country, I could really and truly relax in this wonderful place of peace and quiet.

During the long nights when sleep sometimes didn't come easily, I started to tell the fellow in the next bed about my experiences after I left school to eventually become a gamekeeper on the shores of the Solway.

My next bed neighbour was muffled in more bandages than me

so didn't or couldn't say much, but seemed quite interested and soon requests came from further down the ward to "speak up a bit".

But there was one young fellow in a bed almost opposite mine who had been wheeled in unconscious almost a week previously and had never woken up or spoken a word, until one day a nurse urgently summoned the medical officer with a message that this patient was now in a critical condition.

The MO was a knowledgeable man of few words. All the blankets were immediately removed from the bed, except one that, with a nurse holding each corner, was endlessly flapped up and down in a frantic effort to lower the airman's temperature until the MO decided that, as the young man was breathing normally again, nothing more could be done until he regained consciousness.

In the still of that night this airman suddenly sat up and said, in a clear voice, fully charged with the pent up feelings of someone who had wanted to say something for such a long time, "Jock, tell me again about the wild geese flying across the face of the full moon."

Tree of Knowledge

While the trusty rowan tree safeguards its nearest and dearest, Gideon recalls a very special friend who bit off more than he could chew...

The mountain ash is a small, hardy tree and, true to its name, loves to live and grow in the Highlands.

Its seed is sometimes planted in almost inaccessible, rocky crevices by wild birds who have feasted on the berries of a parent tree.

It's not called the mountain ash in Scotland, bur rowan, or "ruadh-an," red one.

Superstition has also singled it out as a tree with special powers to ward off evil spirits and witches.

That's why you will see a rowan tree, or maybe two, beside the house or farm building of a Highland croft.

It's been purposefully planted to keep the croft from harm by witchcraft and to provide protection from a "puteach," a legendary Gaelic curse which, like the sharp, virulent sting of a wasp, can only be bestowed by the female of the species, usually a witch!

One crofter made no secret of the fact that he had scant regard for superstition and was more than inclined to be a bit on the mean side in his dealings with neighbours and those who worked for him.

He scoffed at the idea of planting a rowan tree to protect his house, until it was rumoured that a woman who had been badly treated in her dealings with him had dared to put a "puteach" on his house.

Not long afterwards, a fork of lightning made a direct hit on his house. It was a near miss for the man, who happened to be in his hay barn at the time.

But the lightning strike left him severely shaken and looking for young rowan trees to plant. And yet they refused to grow near his house.

So he wisely packed his bags and left the building which was later gratefully taken over by a pair of barn owls.

They are birds who are a bit ghost-like themselves in the twilight, but don't care a "twit" or a "to-whoo" about witches.

All this newly-married couple wanted was a place to call home and bring up their family of downy little owls, which they have done so successfully.

Never before have I seen such a bumper crop of rosy-red berries as those that have been hanging in big bunches from the heavily laden rowan trees for the past four or five weeks.

This has set the folk of Strathtummel wondering just what sort of winter weather lies in store for them.

One thing is certain, however - that the harvest of fruit hanging from the rowan trees is a meal that the migrant fieldfares and redwings will really appreciate.

For them, the rowan berries must seem like a lavishly spread table compared to the sparse one they have left behind in Scandinavia.

These birds are ravenously hungry after an ever-so-long strength-sapping flight over the sometimes stormy North Sea.

But the bunches of ripe, succulent rowan berries will be a feast they will talk about for a long time to come.

The fieldfares and redwings belong to the thrush family.

The redwing is the smallest member and, although not an unfriendly bird, has a pronounced dark eye strip which is more than inclined to give it a severe, "keep your distance" look.

As its name suggests, it has blush-red patches on its plumage.

The fieldfare, on the other hand, is much bigger and more boldly marked, with a distinctive silvery-grey head that glistens in the sunshine.

But the fieldfares and the redwings often mingle amicably in a flock together as they constantly search for food.

They are not easily approached, but I understand this, because they are strangers in a strange land, seeking food and friendliness.

That's why I'm currently learning the different phrases in Norwegian, Swedish and Danish for "You're welcome!"

My daughter Valerie, who teaches a class of small children in an Edinburgh school, told me that, apart from gerbils, hamsters and the odd dog or cat, her pupils' knowledge of the bird and animal kingdom was not extensive.

So Valerie bought a goldfish as a pet for the entire class and invited them to christen it with a suitable name.

After a great deal of deliberation, the children decided unanimously that this beautiful little fish should be called Blossom.

I remember when I was a small boy just starting school, a gangling red-haired girl who stayed nearby took me to see her four large goldfish.

They were in the bath, speeding up and down, streaking through the water like gleaming, golden torpedoes.

I was most impressed and was sure my own goldfish, Montague, would appreciate a swim like this, which must seem like crossing the Channel after going round and round in a small glass bowl.

But one thing bothered me, so I asked innocently, "What do you do when you want a bath?"

The red-haired one shrugged her shoulders then, with a shaking fit of giggles that set the curls on her ginger hair dancing up and down, said, "I blindfold them!"

Sometimes Valerie's pupils are treated to an excursion to Edinburgh Zoo so that they can learn as much as possible about all creatures great and small.

I can fully understand the youngsters' feelings.

When I was their age I, too, was taken to the zoo and, in my excitement, leant over to look down into the depths of the sea-lions' pool, when the water suddenly erupted and a face with long, white whiskers, big, brown eyes and breath smelling strongly of fish, gazed at me intently for a second, before trying to take hold of my arm.

It then fell back into the pool with a resounding splash, and the sleeve of my brand new kilt jacket!

Still a bit shaken and wondering when I would get my jacket sleeve back, I found myself being escorted to the first aid post where my wounds - a crescent of toothmarks on my arm - were cauterised.

More importantly, my name was entered in the first aid book as being the first ever bite by a sea-lion.

The word "cauterised" was new to me, but I remembered it well when blatantly showing off my sea-lion bite to all the other schoolboys!

My father later told me that there was a newspaper report saying that the sea-lion had escaped into the Water of Leith.

I knew then that it hadn't really meant me any harm, but just wanted a helping hand in getting back to the wide open spaces and the song of the sea.

Tonight, in the twilight, two barn owls are flitting side by side over the treetops like friendly ghosts.

Their family have now learned to fend for themselves, so the parents are not hunting, just having a carefree night out together.

There's a flock of fieldfares feeding on the berries of the rowan tree purposefully planted to take good care of Croft Douglas. If undisturbed, these birds will be staying for bed and breakfast.

A lady immortalised the mountain ash and its magical powers in a song with such a haunting melody and words that tenderly tug at the heart strings.

"O, rowan tree, O, rowan tree, Thou'lt aye be dear to me."

An Apple A Day

While old timer Drumbuie has something of an uphill struggle, a poacher is left with egg on his face...

Looking out of our bedroom window in the first hazy half-light of a crisp, cool, winter's morning, I can see several Highland cattle climbing the slopes of the steep field that runs up to Croft Douglas from the lochside woods.

Drumbuie, our big-hearted Highland bull, is in the lead, his huge, powerful body sparing no effort to surmount the hill with deliberate, distance-devouring steps.

All this effort reveals itself in twin jets of steam which are puffed out of the big bull's moist, pink nostrils from time to time.

Following behind Drumbuie are the young ones he has adopted - Dorcha, Dileas, Ruraidh, The Bairn and Buie. They, too, are behaving just like little steam trains, filling the icy air above them with long trails of fleecy white frosted breath.

All this and the sight of snow-capped hills sets me thinking that it will soon be time to give the Highland cattle something in the way of a food supplement. Because, although there is a plentiful supply of grass and herbage, especially in the sheltered woods, the growth has lost a lot of its goodness and, like the year itself, become a bit old and tired.

So now is the time to watch that any animal, especially one going to spend the winter outside, doesn't start to lose weight.

A good roly-poly, hairy body provides by far the best blanket for a beastie who has to bed beneath the stars.

The younger cattle have all summered extremely well and won't need anything substantial in the way of supplementary feeding for some weeks yet. But Drumbuie - although we would never say so in front of him - is, shall we say, "getting on a bit".

That's why I keep quietly slipping him all sorts of extras to keep his health and strength up to standard.

Up until now, none of the others seem to have noticed this, except Buie who is Drumbuie's shadow, following him here, there and everywhere, with such a sweet sense of devotion that often leaves me wondering who, exactly, is looking after who!

So little Buie knows full well what's going on, constantly peeking out of the corner of his eye at the big bull being hand-fed with apples that have had their cores completely removed before being stuffed with concentrated vitamin powder, a magical mixture of home-grown herbs and a topping of treacle.

No wonder Drumbuie drools over each delicious offering, before wrapping his huge tongue lovingly around it, then crunching with such satisfaction before finally swallowing.

By this time little Buie is drooling too!

So with my hand held out behind my back so Drumbuie doesn't see me, when I feel the tickle of little Buie's pink tongue on my palm, I slip him one of the apples, hoping he will have the good sense to keep his mouth tight shut and not tell the others.

Drumbuie must have a sweet tooth, because he devours the doctored apples at twice the speed of the potatoes I once used to disguise the powder and feverfew which healed his arthritic foot!

I've changed my "bait" because we have a bumper crop of eating apples at Croft Douglas this year.

For weeks now, Irralee and Shona have been gathering the apple harvest and picking up windfalls from the soft turf of our little orchard.

At the moment, boxes and boxes of sweet dessert apples are being carefully stored in the cool confines of the dairy, whilst the biggest of the windfalls are being fed to Drumbuie.

Windfalls, as their name suggests, are apples which have been shaken from the trees by a boisterous wind and, by all outward appearances, haven't been harmed by it.

But even the bump of a soft landing can cause slight bruising, which means the apple won't keep.

So Shona turned to another of the recipes from the book her great-grandmother had left behind.

Amongst the invaluable advice on its yellowed, well-thumbed pages are detailed handwritten instructions on how to get the most out of windfalls.

When I asked Shona what she was going to do with the masses of chopped apples in the middle of the kitchen, she chuckled in a most mysterious way. Then she confessed that she was going to make the apple mountain into chutney, just as Great-granny did.

This involves making a mixture of chopped apples, still smelling of the summer sun's sweet warm kiss, and bags of sultanas, which bring their own brand of sunshine from a foreign land.

The other ingredients have all been grown in the Croft Douglas garden - finely sliced shallot onions, herbs all blessed with exotic names, and garlic cloves which, when crushed, give off an alluring scent.

Everything is allowed to stew slowly together for some considerable time in subtly blended vinegars.

A little later I had a look through the glass door leading into our kitchen, when I was sure I saw Shona weeping whilst stirring the steaming cauldron of chutney.

So I popped in to see if everything was all right, only to come out again seconds later without uttering a word and my eyes streaming!

I made a vow there and then, to invite everyone that's in need of a good weep to come into the Croft Douglas kitchen the next time Shona is making chutney. Then they can cry their eyes out and, more than likely, feel a lot better for it.

There was something causing a big disturbance in the henhouse this week. I frequently heard the wild flapping of wings and hysterical cackling from the hens, not to mention the constant alarm calls from an extremely agitated cockerel.

Worse still, we have had no new-laid eggs for days, and even the china replicas to encourage the hens to lay have all gone.

I suspected that this was probably the work of a stoat, as they are so clever at bowling eggs in front of them, using only their supple, agile forepaws.

All this set me thinking about the crofter's wife, faced with a similar situation, who cunningly cracked the last egg she had on a flat stone then sprinkled it with pepper.

The stoat duly returned, sampled the egg, sneezed violently, banging its head on the stone in the process, and staggered away.

This gave me an idea, and I drilled a hole in our last hen's egg, blew out the contents and replaced them with lots of mustard liberally laced with black pepper. Then I sealed the hole over again with sticky tape.

Early next morning, just at laying time, I placed the doctored egg in a nest box and by midday it had gone!

Ever since, there has been peace, perfect peace in the Croft Douglas poultry world, with not a sign of the culprit returning.

So, you see, there is something to be said for some old wives' tales.

A Night To Remember

While the sun-kissed heather-clad Hill of the Ptarmigan is a sight to take your breath away, Gideon recalls how a turn in the spotlight left him in the dark...

To "set the heather on fire" is an expression sometimes used to describe the success of something usually designed to have some spectacular effect.

Well, the early morning sunlight does just that almost every day from early August right through to the end of September and, more often than not, well beyond.

The sun sets the heather aglow with a fiery, fluorescent light that, once seen, is never forgotten.

Amazingly enough, the light doesn't lose a fraction of its warm glow, even when wearing a cloak of fleecy cloud. It's as if the bunches of heather have batteries to store excess sunlight and save it for just such a day.

A lady visitor I spoke to last week put it so well when she said solemnly, "it's a sight to just stand and look at, and look at".

There's a beautiful species of game bird who love to live a healthy life, making young heather shoots their staple diet - and how they thrive on them.

These birds are only seen on certain high Scottish peaks, like the one that reaches for the sky on the other side of Loch Tummel, almost directly opposite Croft Douglas.

This particular peak boasts the Gaelic name of "Meall Tarruin Chon" which translates as "Hill of the Ptarmigan".

The ptarmigan stay at the top of the hill all year round and are the only birds in Britain to magically turn their blue-grey summer plumage, so attractively powdered with speckles, to snow-white in the wintertime.

This colouring makes a complete camouflage, and combined with a swift, lightning-like speed of flight, keeps them comparatively safe from human hunters and wild predators alike.

The magnificent, mahogany-coloured red grouse who inhabit the lower slopes love the heather shoots, too.

Their numbers have dwindled in recent years, making the "Glorious Twelfth" of August a thing of the past in this part of the Highlands in the meantime.

Recent reports suggest that carrion crows and foxes from forestry plantations on the nearby hills will also have to be controlled before there is any real improvement in this situation.

I don't let all this get me too down in the dumps, because I know that, in the end, Dame Nature will always have her own way.

After all, she has been looking after the good earth so well for millions of years, and I am sure she will soon sort things out again, just as they should be, helping to give the moors, hills and heather the breathing space that is their heritage.

This will ensure that the honey bees will continue to do a ritual dance when their "scouts" bring back work to the hive that they have found the best of the heather blooms.

They will then show the host of worker bees exactly where to go by performing an exciting points-of-the compass waltz.

After which, the entire working population of the hive takes off in a cloud that momentarily darkens the sky, buzzing with the exciting news of knowing exactly where they are going and what for!

They have a tender approach to the sensitive heather flowers, humming a sweet, persuasive song whilst tentatively stroking the bell-like petals to seek admittance.

When this is granted, the bee reaches the very heart of the bloom to gain a bounteous gift of nectar.

Before leaving, the bee makes a small return gesture by taking pollinating messages to neighbouring flowers.

It then flies back to the hive, heavily laden with the ingredients to make rich, dark heather honey, which to my mind deserves the title, "Food of the Gods".

For quite a few years I performed at the Highland Nights held in Pitlochry Recreation Park, to entertain the tourists who came to Perthshire and to raise funds for our world-famous Vale of Atholl Pipe Band.

As the summer came to an end and the nights began to draw in, the final Highland Nights were always floodlit.

I found this time to be the most exciting of all, performing under blazing arc lights which revealed me, and what I did, in every detail, to the crowded amphitheatre with its high terracing and treble circle of cars and coaches.

I, however, couldn't see a thing and, like a Roman gladiator, apprehensively awaited some sign as to how the multitudes had received my efforts.

Would there be a silence in the darkness, I often wondered, or was someone possibly planning to throw something!

But my fears were groundless, and the thunderous applause and constant tooting of car horns spelled out success, and went to my head like wine.

On occasion, there was also an impromptu incident that brought the house down - like the blind Irish girl who won the "lucky programme number" competition.

When she joined me under the arc lights to receive her prize, I was struck by her beautiful, untroubled face.

As we spoke together into the microphone, the girl lightly stroked my velvet doublet with her fingertips.

"Ah, sure," she said, with such an attractive Irish brogue. "You fell so soft and warm, just like my dear little donkey back in County Down!"

I can't manage to attend many Highland Nights and ceilidhs at the moment because there is so much to do, looking after the croft and its livestock.

But sometimes, with Irralee's invaluable help, I act as compere at some extra-special ceilidhs, such as the one I did not so long ago.

There, a charming English lady told me how much she had enjoyed herself, because the ceilidh had helped her to forget about the medical problem that was worrying her - if only for the evening.

This same lady called at Croft Douglas some weeks ago to tell me joyfully, "You said I would be all right when the heather bloomed".

And the sunlight danced in her eyes as she added, "I just had to call to tell you how right you were!"

It's a lesson I have learned in life, to lift my eyes to the hills - especially when the heather is in bloom.

Monarch Of The Glen

While Gideon remembers words of wisdom from his mother,
a titanic struggle is taking place in the hills around Croft
Douglas...

For some days now, especially in the stillness of a rosy red
sunset and just before the darkness comes down, there's a spine-
chilling sound to be heard, echoing and re-echoing around the
rocky peaks of the purple heathered hills.

It's a sound that can only be compared to the full-throated roars
of forest-bred lions claiming to be the King of Beasts.

But these aren't lions, they're Britain's biggest wild animals -
fully-grown red deer stags, wearing regal crowns that entitle them
to constantly challenge each other in almost endless, no holds
barred, antler clashing, foot flailing fights, to prove which one of
them has the right to rule a purple heather-clad kingdom, high in
the hills.

The big stags battle strenuously with heaving, russet red flanks
flecked with foam, sparing no effort and giving everything they
have, to prove, decisively, that they are indeed the best of their
breed!

What a prize the winner will gain! He will have the undisputed
right to wear Royal and Imperial coronets and will have the red
deer's most coveted title, Monarch of the Glen. And, probably the
most important of all, he will have a harem of beautiful red deer
hinds who have admired all the hard fought conquests from a
respectable distance and are now his devoted slaves.

But all this beauty, that has been so hard to fight for, now places
a heavy burden of responsibility on the broad shoulders of the

17

Monarch. He, and he alone, must look after all the ladies and continually circle around his would-be wives because, with all the wiles and wisdom of femininity, they will only grant him their favours when they are good and ready to do so.

This leaves the Monarch with no option but to continue travelling round and round with scarcely time to snatch a mouthful of hill grass or heather, just in case he should miss the moment when female eyelids are lowered demurely in consent to his desire.

He must also be on guard to catch the sight of another big stag he has already beaten in battle, who is lurking somewhere in the shadows, still hoping to gain some slight revenge to soothe his deeply wounded pride by finding a wayward hind who has seen his handsome form from the distance and purposefully, step by grazing step, strayed away from the others.

As the Monarch grows leaner and becomes just a shadow of his former, magnificent, self, how he must look forward to the day when all his wives will be happily carrying his children. Because that's when the oldest hind with the most experience, will "take over" the leadership of the herd and, when winter lays its icy hand over the land, lead them down from the snow-covered mountains to where there is shelter and food among the silver birch trees below.

The mushrooms have gradually finished growing, but their memory is kept fresh until another year by the bottle of ketchup that, almost permanently, takes pride of place on the Croft Douglas table at meal times.

But it's now the toadstools' turn to take over and this year, as the mushrooms did, they are putting on a display such as I have never seen before.

In the hours between the dusk of one day to the dawn of another, they fill the fields full of different designs and colours, working their way to lay a colourful carpet through the woods, then climbing right up the hills as far as they can go to mingle with, and brighten up, the fading hill grass and heather blooms.

I have friends who gather the golden chanterelle and extol their qualities as a delicacy of the highest order. They also pick Puff Balls, almost as big as footballs, and drool over them when thinly sliced and fried in butter.

All this doesn't make me deviate, though, from my mum's teaching that all good-to-eat mushrooms grow in open fields, far away from trees, are snow white on the top with blush pink gills underneath. The ultimate test, Mother always insisted, was that the top skin on the dome of the mushroom peeled off easily and its pink gills should have a friendly, never-to-be forgotten smell.

I hate to think how many would-be experimenters slipped away in their sleep after taking a "Destroying Angel".

Even the Emperor Claudius is credited with having done this when sampling "Death Cap" at supper time.

Who, I wonder, would ever want to spread their bread with "Witches' Butter" or, worse still, partake of a portion of "Stinkhorn" or be up all night after eating the "Sickener".

So I definitely leave the edible fungi decisions to the experts and stay with what I have been told "mushroomwise" because, I too, like my mum, am passionately fond of mushrooms and make no mistakes when picking them!

The most colourful toadstools I have ever seen grow on the broad shoulders of Creag Mhor, the hill that rises up behind Croft Douglas.

So, the other evening, I climbed to see them when the sun was setting, because that's when toadstools look at their magical best.

I had almost reached the rocky shoulder of the Creag when I was suddenly rooted to the spot by a loud, nerve-shattering roar, so close as to set my teeth chattering.

It was a royal stag who must have mistaken me for a rival trying to infiltrate his territory. I immediately "froze" beside a small birch tree and could hear my heart beating wildly as the big stag studied me with lowered antlers, bloodshot eyes and wide, flaring nostrils that made a snorting noise like a surfacing whale.

I could only think of the time my grandfather, Gideon, told me that his father had suffered serious injury in an attack from a rutting stag, and wondered if I were about to meet a similar fate.

Fortunately for me, just at that moment, there was an excited "bark" from a hind who was somewhere on the crest of Creag Mhor. Without hesitation, the big stag spun round and charged uphill, crashing his way through the birch tree branches.

There was no doubt in the Monarch's mind what was happening. In his temporary absence, a beaten rival, hoping to avenge himself, was having an affair with one of the ladies from his harem.

Which left me with the thought that it's a wise little red deer fawn that knows his own father!

With a sigh of relief, I was slipping silently downhill when, right at my feet, I saw a ring of toadstools in various shades of iridescent red, studded with little luminous white spots.

I would never be tempted to pick them, not for all the tea in China!

Besides, they are, more than probably, fairy furnishings for an especial occasion, like a Little People's Party and I wouldn't for anything in the world, offend the Fairies.

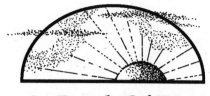

At Break Of Day

This year's crop of snow-white mushrooms made a sumptuous feast for both animals and humans alike - and the fairies didn't go short either!

Life in this beautiful part of the Scottish Highlands has so many unaccountable happenings and innumerable tales told about "The Fairies" that in time, if you weren't before, you find yourself becoming a "believer".

There are folk who have lived here all their lives who seem to understand the strange signs and unexplained action of The Fairies.

All the year round the "believers" go out of their way to please the "little people" who, they are certain, can bring lots of lick, not necessarily money-wise, but the blessing of Good Health.

That's why, at the end of every year, The Fairies' friends show their thanks by planning a big party for the little people, placing a feast of good things on the doorstep of their homes just before the clock strikes twelve, to announce the magic moments of Hogmanay.

Sure enough, when the dawn then sets another New Year alight with the promise of sunshine, all the saucers of hand-baked shortbread and blackcurrant bun are polished clean, without even a left-over crumb.

That's a sure sign that it will be a healthy, happy New Year for the donor who really believes.

I know of at least one lady "believer" and annual visitor, who from a bedroom window at the break of day, continually contrives to catch The Fairies on film.

One morning, I thought to take a picture of our handsome,

young, Maran cockerel's first brood of chickens which are now growing up to be very beautiful birds, when suddenly I saw a golden, glowing light bordered by a bright red circle, floating just above the blackthorn bushes.

So I raised the camera lens and snapped it, but was most disappointed when I moved closer to find only the speckled Maran chickens.

There are also different signs, almost left purposefully, to show you and anyone else who pauses to have a closer look that "They" have been around. There are also the unexplained circles that appear, overnight, in the hay or corn crops that look as if they could have been caused by baby rabbits playfully chasing each other round and round, or dainty little roedeer trotting nose to tail, only there's no sign of a roadway in, or out!

The circles always look so perfect, as if created by precision instruments. I like to think that they could be caused by The Fairies holding hands and dancing by moonlight in a ring.

What a harvest of mushrooms there has been this year, covering the fields in the morning, with what looks like a heavy fall of fast-melting snow.

Besides being a seasonal luxury for humans, the animals find mushrooms an extremely tasty bite, too.

They are especially sought after by the small field or wood mouse who spends a lot of time foraging in the fields when the weather is at its kindest.

Then, at the first sign of hard frost, you'll find it scurrying as fast as its little legs will go for shelter under the trees and whatever has been stored beneath the blanket of fallen leaves.

The bunny rabbits believe in leading much the same kind of lifestyle and love to hop in and out of the mushroom rings, while having many a nibble at this savoury meal.

Cattle and sheep, too, all have a hankering to make mushrooms an exciting additive to a browsing breakfast.

If you wish a share of this sumptuous feast, you have to be a little bit more than just an "occasional early riser".

The wee field mice wearing their warm, velvety waistcoats and the bunny rabbits, with their fur coats, have been running about long before the dawn's early light.

But they have just been "sampling and nibbling," so it's best to be out and about before the sheep and cattle begin their wholesale munching.

They grow best on the lower, more fertile lochside land and a very profitable plan is to put some bronzed bracken on top of the "tiny buttons" not yet ready for picking. This will keep them temporarily concealed from prying eyes and ensure that the "bigger beasties," who don't like the taste of dry bracken, won't touch them.

The mushrooms will poke their big, circular, snow white heads up through the bracken by the following morning when you must gather them before anyone, or anything, else does!

But what are we to do with this colossal crop of mushrooms?

Youngest daughter, Shona, having got hold of Great Granny's faded cook book containing recipes for "super sauces" found one that seemed to solve the situation.

Once Shona has made up her mind to do something, it just has to happen. Big, deep, earthenware bowls were filled with purposefully bruised mushrooms, each layer suitably salted with a slight sensation of black pepper, before adding yet another layer on top, and stirred daily for a Highland week, around five days.

After this the mass of melting mushrooms are baked for five hours in a "slow oven" then herbs, cloves, a trace of ginger root and a bottle of the best red wine are used as additives.

Then it is strained and boiled to reduce and strengthen the liquid, whilst subtle aromatic smells of the dark, exotic, mushroom mixture has everyone drooling.

Before being finally bottled, it was first tested on mince and tatties, always a favourite meal. The taste was so delicious that everyone asked for more!

I always wondered, when I was a small boy and had graduated to sit at the dining table, why all the adults, whatever the meal, gleefully passed the sauce bottle round and round to savour a sprinkle or two of Granny's Mushroom Ketchup.

The Great Escape

While the ebb and flow of Loch Tummel allows the livestock to become "free range", there's an anxious moment when Drumbuie goes missing...

All the money we had so carefully saved to ensure a financial solution to any future emergency was spent this year renewing miles of fencing.

This was to make sure that our livestock didn't stray from Croft Douglas land, especially the Highland cattle who, like the wild red and roe deer, live their lives outside, whatever the weather, all year round.

So it was something of a shock when the waters of Loch Tummel which, with the aid of a fresh west wind, frequently overlap their designated meeting place with Croft Douglas land, were suddenly doing the reverse and receding.

This meant that our Highland cattle had to walk a bit further to slake their thirst, only to find that there was now a new narrow pathway to the west along which they could proceed, in single file, with the long hairs on the back of their necks bristling with the excitement of possible adventure in pastures new.

That's why the beginning of this week saw me building a barricade down to the new water level in an attempt to prevent any further wanderings.

So it was with a great sense of apprehension that, from a hiding place in the hazel trees, I watched the Highlanders come down to the loch for a drink and sniff suspiciously as they inspected the newly-built barricade.

Finally, they blew down their nostrils in a Gaelic expression of frustration, before turning back to the lochside field, snatching some succulent grass tussocks for supper and, one by one, bedding down for the night.

On Saturday, our telephone rang - a single, sharp alarm call that really made me sit up and take notice.

It was Robin, from his lochside croft to the west, saying that my cattle had wandered up the loch again and were making their way to the main road.

We now needed all the help available, because we knew that traffic is always busiest at the weekend.

John and Carol from Borenich are neighbours who know what a situation like this is all about and were on the scene within minutes.

With Robin and his daughter's help, we located the cattle and guided them towards the section of road where John and Carol were waiting to halt the traffic before setting off, fleet-footed, in front of the herd to warn any oncoming cars, whilst Irralee and Shona kept the beasties moving from behind.

I was last of all, walking alongside a crawling car that seemed to enjoy going slowly.

So I had plenty of time to study the sole occupant, a lady with long hair that flowed effortlessly over her shoulders in chestnut-coloured waves.

She appeared to be holding an animated conversation with herself, but this came as no great surprise to me, as Irralee sometimes does this, too.

I don't think I do, but this could probably be because people who know otherwise haven't plucked up sufficient courage to tell me!

The lady wound down her car window, revealing a honey-coloured complexion, lit up by bright shining eyes that looked surprisingly sane.

She thoughtfully invited me to "hop in and have a lift". So I climbed into the passenger seat while the lady continued to converse with herself.

I watched the Highlanders' hairy bottoms bobbing about in front of the leading car, and Irralee keeping everything moving in a most orderly fashion, reproving both impatient drivers and wayward Highlanders with a warning wave of her little hazel wand.

I soon found out that the lady who had given me a lift wasn't in fact having a word with the fairies, as I had thought.

She introduced herself as Linda, an author from Australia, and added, "Please don't mind the tape recorder. I'm collecting material for my book".

I said "So long" to Linda, expressing the hope that her book would be a great success.

The stray Highlanders were now safely secured in the paddock we keep for emergencies, where the lush grass is seldom grazed.

But we have to search on for Drumbuie, our big, beloved Highland bull, who is still missing.

It was Shona who found him, lying flat out on the wet sand, close to the lapping water.

Drumbuie had seemingly slipped and fallen when trying to follow the others, who had waded around the barrier when the water went back further still.

Together, Shona and I struggled mightily to help him to his feet, then found that Drumbuie had injured a foreleg.

So, step by tortuous step, we persuaded the big bull to limp with his damaged leg, up the steep hill from the lochside to the comfort and company of the others in the paddock.

Sadly, the birds who would have warned us about all this man-made meddling with the loch water have all gone back to the sea-shore for the winter - the redshank with its shrill, piping alarm, the oyster-catcher screaming, "be quick, be quick", and the one I miss most of all, the musical, soulful calling of the curlew.

Fare You Well!

Having covered up their tracks, the nimble squirrels play hide and seek and go in search of a treasure trove, reminding Gideon of a canny man, for whom a transatlantic trip became an errand of mercy...

A promise made is a debt unpaid, and primroses, for me, are plants that always keep a promise.

Even during the winter's hardest days, when their long leaves lie flattened and frozen under sheets of ice and blankets of snow, the primrose plants still retain those vital glints of green, promising that, some day, tiny frondy fingers will reach out of their hearts with handfuls of gold.

Gifts for everyone from the good earth to bring endless pleasure and provide sunshine on the dullest day, the primrose plants perform this service every year all by themselves, without any outside aid.

Unlike some other floral arrangements that appear in the most unexpected places, they make me pause for more than a moment to marvel at those masterpieces created by creatures like the little red squirrels.

How industriously they spend all their spare time burying fir cones, hazelnuts, rowan and alder berries.

It's an inborn instinct, a legacy left to them by their ancestors, a recipe for survival when the woodlands are caught in the creeping icy clutch of winter.

Fortunately for everyone, the red squirrels always seem to fear the worst when it comes to facing up to winter, and before the leaves are falling from the trees, they begin to bury stores of supplies in all sorts of places, to stave off starvation and see them and their families safely through until spring.

They successfully plan ahead, only to forget where they had buried all this food in the first place!

Then they often find that the winter weather wasn't so bad after all and that all the nuts, seeds and berries they had so shrewdly put away "for a snowy day" are about to become little trees that will take their place in the woodlands and, in time, help to provide the wildlife with food when it's needed most.

All the folk in the glen called Robin "The Squirrel" because he was a crofter who hoarded things that seemed somehow "special" to him.

Whenever he went "abroad," it was to Aberfeldy, Perth, Stirling or Oban to sell his blackfaced sheep or Highland cattle.

If, at the end of the day, the sale had been a successful one and he found himself with some money to spare, Robin always found time to browse around the antique shops in town and purchase something he was sure would bring pleasure and be well worth storing.

Robin's wife was called Jenny, which was appropriate in a way because, as far back as I can remember, the robin's mate was mistakenly supposed to be a Jenny Wren.

They were even written about and paired together as the Robin and the Wren when, in reality, a robin's mate looks like a replica of himself, only not so bold and with a somewhat shyer approach and every feather preened to perfection, denoting femininity.

And indeed the tiny Jenny Wren would never dream of choosing a robin for a mate, preferring a more masterful replica of herself.

However, Robin's wife, Jenny, although almost driven to distraction by her husband's compulsive urge to collect, still loved him dearly and wouldn't do anything to make him think otherwise.

They had an only daughter called Ruth, a pretty girl whom Robin and Jenny were so proud of.

She was such a help around the house and the croft, as Ruth had a way with animals that made working with them easy.

Then Ruth was courted by a handsome Canadian who was on holiday in the Highlands and, in a whirlwind romance, he claimed her as his beautiful bride and took her back to Canada with him.

Whilst Robin and Jenny were overjoyed to see Ruth so happy and realised that their fledgling was ready to leave the nest, Jenny wasn't at all sure about the possibility of never seeing her darling daughter again.

Jenny loved to have her supper in bed and Robin knew exactly what to bring her - the "heel" of a wholemeal loaf, liberally spread with strawberry jam, a sweet biscuit sitting beside it and a cup of hot chocolate, made with milk.

When Robin was ready to go to bed, too, he crept upstairs with the silent step of a house mouse because Jenny always went to sleep first and he didn't want to disturb her.

But tonight she woke with a start and threw her arms around Robin, sobbing, "I miss her so much, Why did she have to go such a long way away?"

Robin put his arm round Jenny comfortingly and promised, with his hand on his heart, to give her question his deepest thought and undivided attention.

Whereupon, Jenny sighed and fell asleep, leaving Robin wide awake all night, tossing and turning and wondering what on earth to do.

Worse was till to come.

The next morning, Danny, the postman, delivered an air mail letter from Ruth with a plea to her mother to come as soon as possible to see her brand new granddaughter, adding, "She's just like you, Mum".

Jenny clasped Robin's hand in a grip that wordlessly said, "I've just got to go".

So Robin surveyed his collection and selected an Highland chieftain's dirk, mounted with a large silver thistle topped off with a brilliant sky-blue amethyst for its flower.

Lower down, lodged in the sheath, were a silver knife and fork, the distinctive mark of a man who never ate with his fingers.

After the Friday Market in Perth, at which he wasn't buying but selling, Robin found to his great surprise that his purchase of seven pounds so many years ago had multiplied into a payment of seven hundred!

Robin raced home with the wonderful news that Jenny could catch the first available flight to Canada and all her wildest dreams came true when she hugged her beloved daughter and held the chubby granddaughter made in the same mould as herself.

I saw a red squirrel today.

He was sitting on a tree stump that was surrounded by emerald-green moss and pink willow herb, with wood violets peeping out in colourful posies.

Fairylike ferns curled around the weatherworn lines of bark, caressing every wrinkle, while adventurous fungi had built tiers of matching tea-tables up each side to provide a party place for the Schiehallion fairies.

The squirrel saw me but didn't move.

He knew I meant him no harm and continued to bury a store of seeds, nuts and berries in the old tree stump's rich, peaty centre.

The red squirrel, in his own way, was giving the old tree stump wealth untold, so that some day, not so very far away, the world would beat a path to this old stump, now transformed into a magnificent tree once more, and marvel at so much beauty from such a small beginning.

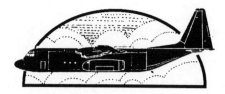

Up, Up And Away

The sudden arrival of some boisterous interlopers is a shock to the system for the Strath's wildlife but, for her part, Irralee is transported...

Irralee has been "horse-daft" since, at six years old, she sat on her first pony.

From then on, as she grew up, the ponies continued to correspond in size and Irralee found herself, as a schoolgirl spending her precious pocket money on her pets and then, when a teenager, found that clothing allowances went the same way on oats and hay.

All this for the sake of keeping her beloved pony and the abounding pleasure it brought her.

Irralee, I'm sure, often wondered with knitted brows why she hadn't been born a boy in the first place!

That would have made everything so easy, because she could have enlisted as a Junior Trooper in the Royal Scots Greys and been sent to their exclusive riding school at Weedon for detailed instruction in the finer points of horsemanship.

She did, however, eventually manage to talk her way into Redford Barracks where the Greys were stationed, as a special guest.

While she learnt a lot during her visit, at the same time she helped to sort out some of their problems with awkward animals.

Funnily enough, the "feminine touch" seems to have a far more calming, reassuring influence over a horse than a masculine movement which seems to lack the fingertip sensitiveness that is often so essential.

However, in time, Irralee "went off" the Royal Scots Greys when the War Office, in their wisdom, decided that modern warfare made horses redundant.

So the troopers took their highly-trained "saddle seats" to sit crouched in huge tanks, armed to the teeth.

Not that Irralee disagreed with the War Office decision as such. She was all in favour of withdrawing any animal from a dangerous situation.

To her, horses are a way of life, pieces of poetry constructed to blend with bone and muscle, covered with a soft, silken skin supporting delicate dancing legs and a gaily-carried, long silver tail flowing like a waterfall.

And although Irralee loves all horses, they should preferably have the dished face of an aristocratic Arab, with kindly dark brown eyes looking out through a screen of snow-white eyelashes.

Whilst out on her daily ride around Croft Douglas on Kahli, who, in Irralee's estimation, is a King in the horse world, she has discovered a new delight - "plane spotting".

There is plenty of opportunity for this as Loch Tummel was selected as a perfect place for the Royal Air Force to practise the fine art of low-level flying.

"Isn't it all so exciting!" Irralee exclaimed. "And Kahli seems to enjoy it, too".

"He just stands stock still and waggles his ears while I wave to the airmen".

Which all made me wonder what effect this activity in the air would be having on the wildlife of Lochtummelside.

Amazingly enough, the first time the low-flying planes came over, it was our herd of Highland cattle that "took off" with their tails in the air.

But they soon realised that this aerial intruder meant no harm to them and, in the days that followed, like the roe deer and the rabbits, they only raised their heads to watch the planes as they swept overhead with a high-pitched scream.

Then, like the calm after a storm, the huge Hercules aircraft came flying in formation up the loch to perform their own particular exercises.

They didn't disturb anyone or anything. In fact, on a hazy summer afternoon, the lazy, droning lullaby of their engines gave everything the urge to seek a shady spot and relax.

And no wonder, for they are the gentle giants of the air.

Unarmed, without any weapon of destruction, their main task is to support troop movements and alleviate the suffering of sick and starving humans anywhere on earth, twenty-four hours a day, seven days a week.

Their motto is simply, "Support, save and supply".

Irralee was fascinated by the beauty of the giant Hercules and its gentle approach, sounding just like a big bumble bee hunting for honeysuckle.

She left all the doors of the house open, so that nothing would hinder her sudden dash outside when the distant humming of the Hercules came sounding up the valley. She would wave whatever came to hand, usually a tea towel, but I ventured to suggest that if she wanted to attract the attentions of any aircrew, all that was required was a pair of silk stockings, because the pilots I used to know proudly wore their wife's or girlfriend's stockings like a silk scarf, something like a lucky charm.

I couldn't help wondering what had happened to those romantic notions when silk stockings had been replaced by a tea towel!

But, amazingly enough, Irralee's signals seemed to have been received and understood, resulting in an invitation to Leuchars in Scotland and Lyneham in Wiltshire, where Irralee, who had never flown before, found herself on the flight deck of a Hercules, high in the sky.

And it didn't end there.

Irralee was then collected from Croft Douglas by a Hercules crew to participate in dropping exercises on Rannoch Moor. How vital these practice drops have proved when the Hercules are weaving their way around mountain tops to help refugees in a faraway land.

Today dawned as every summer's day does on Loch Tummel, with a change of scenery.

The mountains had just shrugged off the shrouds of mist clinging around their shoulders and, with the warmth of the sun caressing the corners of every cold crag, they gazed down at their reflections in the mirror of the motionless water.

Irralee had spent weeks of waiting without a plane in sight, but her luck was about to change, and this morning there was a steady drone like the murmuring of a queen bee, growing in volume and coming from the west.

We were in the middle of a meal, but Irralee rose and, totally regardless of the chaos caused to the crockery, she grabbed the tablecloth and raced outside, waving it wildly!

The Hercules waggled its wings in response, then turned to swoop low over Irralee's head, to give her the thrill of a lifetime as she listened to the gigantic pulsating propellers singing together in close harmony, "We just called to say 'we're home'."

Spare A Thought

As Gideon takes to the road, he knows to keep a watchful eye open for some "cross country" travellers, but he's not prepared for one or two astonishing encounters...

The road to Strathtummel is like the one through life, with many twists and turns and a multitude of breathtaking bends, before it straightens out in between.

Then there's a fair share of steep braes to surmount with, fortunately, far more joys than sorrows.

If it's beauty you're looking for, this road is where you only have to lift your eyes to enjoy the feast of a lifetime.

If, for some reason or another, I have to visit Pitlochry when the tourist season is at its peak, I make a point of going early in the morning, doing what has to be done and getting back as quickly as possible to the peace and quiet of Strathtummel. But not too quickly.

The most important thing on any journey, especially at this time of day, is to keep a sharp lookout for birds and animals crossing.

They don't have sophisticated sets of traffic lights with little green men signalling when it's safe to go!

The wild ones go whenever they want, which can be anywhere at anytime, with a frightening disregard for fast motor cars.

By far the fastest to cross is a low-flying bird, its beak crammed with caterpillars, carrying much needed food for a second brood of hungry young ones.

It only takes a quick, instinctive step on the footbrake to ensure she has a safe crossing, and a future for her family.

Then there are the baby bunnies, born at the roadside, who are making their first exciting exploration of the outside world.

They bounce back and forward and can't quite make up their minds whether to cross or not, so they have to be treated with great care.

The red squirrel is different. Its mind is made up from the start, and it makes a lightning dash across the road, its tail streaming out behind, in an all-out effort to reach its favourite crop of fir cones on the other side.

But this morning I am in for a big surprise just after rounding the bend to the east of Borenich Farm. For standing in the middle of the road is the smallest roe deer fawn I have ever seen - not a fraction more than nine inches in height!

A quick glance in my rearview mirror tells me that the school bus is not far behind and, approaching at a steady pace from the front, there's a huge wood lorry bound for the forest to pick up timber.

By now I have stopped in front of the tiny, fragile fawn with my car hazard lights working overtime.

I can't think how this little one came to be there all alone because it's obviously only a few hours old. But there's no time for speculation.

"Uncle George", who knows this road and the wanderings of wildlife so well, has drawn his bus to an immediate stop. Meanwhile the wood lorry driver, who's probably no stranger to the Strathtummel road either, brings his lorry to a hissing halt with his hydraulic brakes.

Both Uncle George and the lorry driver have the good sense to turn off their engines, so the silence is only broken by a chaffinch singing a carefree song from the top of a silver birch tree as I slowly approach this ever-so-dainty roe deer.

The tiny fawn turned to me with huge, staring eyes and began to bleat a baby cry, "Be-ah, be-ah, be-ah," just like a little newborn lamb trying out its voice for the first time.

The temptation to lift this little one and give it a reassuring cuddle before carrying it to the side of the road, and so swiftly resolving the whole situation, is very strong.

But that would never do.

It might break the precious bond between mother and child, because the little fawn might get mixed up between my scent and its mother's and wonder which one to follow.

Worse than that, Mother might get the idea that her child had been contaminated by this strange human smell and she might desert it.

So I quietly and slowly shepherded this dainty little piece of living beauty back to the side of the road where it tottered briefly on top of the grassy bank, then slid down to settle in a small bed of bracken.

I felt that, for the time being, it would be safe there from the perils of road traffic, and so I sprinted back to my car.

Uncle George and the lorry driver restarted their engines and gave me cheery, understanding waves as I drove away.

On my return journey, I couldn't help but wonder how the tiny fawn was. At least I knew that, because of its size, there was no way it could scramble up the steep bank and back on to the road.

I would have liked to stop where I left it and have a quick look, but the road was getting busy now and I didn't wish to create a situation that would attract well-meaning tourists with cameras.

So I drove on and kept my secret, little knowing there was yet another surprise waiting for me just around the last bend before Croft Douglas.

As I pulled up, there was pandemonium among the jackdaw colony that nests around the rocky crags of Creag Mhor, the high hill that rises to reach for the sky at the back of our house.

It was all the fault of a pair of peregrine falcons.

They were busy giving aerial displays for the benefit of their four fully-fledged youngsters, teaching them to fold their wings, fall like a stone through the air and strike their target with extended talons.

The young peregrines were having a great deal of fun practising diving down on the jackdaws.

They weren't doing any real damage, but the parent jackdaws were taking a very poor view of the whole procedure and protesting vociferously.

When I went to see what was going around Creag Mhor, it seemed to be just as I had thought, a lot of noise about nothing. But, fluttering weakly in a bunch of bell heather, was a beautiful bird.

At first sight I thought it was a rock dove, struck down by falcons. But I had wronged the peregrines.

They had only been playing with the jackdaws and this bird was a completely exhausted homing pigeon.

These usually have a feathering of subtle pale blue with dark shadows, black bars on their wings and a distinctive fall of snow at the base of their beaks.

I do know there can be other colourings, but this bird was definitely different, with the blush of a sunset seeping through the breast feathers, and wearing what looked like a large white snowflake as a crown on its head.

I picked up the pigeon carefully, folding its long, tapering wings, and carried it back to Croft Douglas.

There I put it in the henhouse, where there was fresh water to drink and food in the form of golden wheat grains and kibbled maize.

I had a peak later that night and was pleased to see the pigeon and our handsome Maran cockerel sitting closely, side by side, fast asleep.

We call our cockerel Snowy Owl because of his pristine white plumage laced with strands of gold.

I'm so glad he has taken this tired and lost little pigeon under his protective wing for tonight.

I'll Be Back

Gideon attends to some unfinished business along the Strathtummel road, while the departure of a new-found friend is a bittersweet experience...

The Snowy Owl, our magnificent Maran cockerel, woke me this morning with his first crow.

Sometimes it takes a series of his strident clarion calls to shake the sleep from my eyes, but that is only when there are no persistent thoughts continually knocking at the door of my mind.

This morning, the thoughts I slipped off to sleep with returned refreshed, to remind me about the little lost roe deer that I had shepherded to what I was sure would be a safe spot.

Had I piloted the small roe to the right place, where its mother was almost certain to find and cuddle it? Or was the tiny fawn lying there, all alone, a prey to any passing predator?

Then there's the homing pigeon I found lying in an exhausted bundle by a bunch of bell heather on the hill. But I took it home and left it in the byre with food, water and the Snowy Owl, who is first class at caring for any new member of his feathered flock.

So I quickly decided to make the fragile fawn my first priority.

Ceilidh, my little spaniel, doesn't take a lot of wakening. She knows full well that something is on my mind and that I have decided to take her along with me.

Because of her sensitive nose, Ceilidh can detect and differentiate between the smell of anyone or anything, long before they can even be seen or heard by me.

We set off together down the Strathtummel road. The day is barely five hours old and everything is glistening with drops of morning dew.

Baby rabbits are bobbing about everywhere.

How they love exploring this huge, wide world, which is so much bigger than their burrow, and contains so many good thing to eat.

Yet, even at this young age, they have the instinct to quickly follow the first flash of a white tail and heed the warning "thump" of a hind foot from those who think they have spotted something sinister.

So they all scurry back to the safety of their burrows.

I looked around, wondering what the baby bunnies had seen that sent them running for home in such a hurry. Could it have been the big bird, high overhead, winging its way back to the loch?

It's an osprey that has probably travelled from a tree-top nest near the Loch of the Lowes.

The osprey wouldn't have bothered the little bunnies, however.

Fish is this bird's favourite food, and I feel sure that the only thing on its mind at this moment is the concentration and skill required to catch a Tummel trout!

Now I can just see the silvery back of a big boar badger as he bustles his way through the thick bracken of a deep ditch.

The badger is mainly nocturnal and is quickly making his way home before the day gets any lighter.

Home, for him, lies on the gentle slopes of Creag Mhor under a big rock, and has a huge hole for a front door screened by bunches of bell heather.

I know this because one evening as darkness was falling I saw the badger evicting a fox who was trying to take up tenancy in his house.

A badger's set is an elaborately constructed, many-roomed mansion, with a special bedroom for the lady of the house, lined with layers of bronzed bracken.

These "blankets" and other furnishings are renewed whenever required with fresh material because badgers are very houseproud creatures.

We weren't far away from the place where I had shepherded the tiny lost fawn to safety.

Ceilidh confirmed this by suddenly freezing with one forepaw suspended in mid-air and her soft, creamy-white muzzle dappled with dark blue spots pointing straight ahead to a big silver birch tree with its branches draped down to touch the ground.

Sheltering there, next to the birch tree's silver body and behind the screen of its small heart-shaped leaves, I could just see a russet-red roe deer. I immediately recognised the beautiful little fawn, suckling safely at its mother's side.

It only took a split second to allow my mind to make this moment one to remember for ever, before Ceilidh and I turned quietly around and slipped away.

Then we both hurried back to Croft Douglas to see how the stray homing pigeon I had found on the hill was faring, after "Bed and Breakfast" in the henhouse!

First of all I had a peek through the window and saw the pigeon feeding happily with the hens.

They are quite used to other birds sharing their breakfast, especially the flocks of colourful chaffinches who bring their families with them - even late babies still wearing their first flight feathers, who haven't even passed a "flying test".

They are still wearing the yellow "elastic bands" at each side of their baby beaks, which allow them to open really wide when their parents pop some food in.

I suppose they should all be foraging far and wide at this time of year when food is plentiful, but they do fully repay whatever is eaten in the henhouse by having such a wonderful choir of songsters.

The pigeon stopped eating when I opened the door and tip-toed daintily towards me.

It was then that I made up my mind, because of her beauty and shy mannerisms, that she probably belonged to the fair sex. I also decided that, because of the white crown of fine feathers on her head, she just had to be called Snowdrop.

Whilst Snowdrop sat on my wrist and picked out some golden kibbled maize from the palm of my hand, I studied the rubber ring around her leg. Printed boldly on it was the name Bill Smith and a telephone number.

A soft west-coast voice answered my call and was so pleased to hear that I had found his lost homing pigeon.

Bill confirmed my suspicion that it was a very young bird blown far away by a sudden gale on its first flight and not really old enough to find its way back.

But Bill finished on a bright note and told me there was a very efficient service for returning pigeons who, for one reason or another, had lost their way home, and that he would be in touch with them right away.

He rang again the next morning, to say that a courier would call at midday to collect Snowdrop.

The Pigeon Express was right on time and the courier, cheerfully efficient, prepared a special box for Snowdrop, and made a note of her name with particulars and time of her departure point and destination.

It was with real regret that I handed over this beautiful bird and realised in the moment of parting how fond I had grown of her.

However, I was so pleased that she was going back to where she belonged because I firmly believe, for person or pigeon, there really is no place like home.

The Gathering Place

In winter, the locals congregate on the frozen Loch Kinardochy, which has long been a very special meeting place...

We never think of winter as a season of the year that comes on particular calendar months, unlike spring, summer and autumn, which sometimes have a hiccup, but still manage to make an appearance more or less when they are supposed to.

Winter, on the other hand, is a law unto itself, the most arrogant season of all, and can blow a bitter north-east breath with a biting blizzard of snow early in October, or keep everyone guessing for weeks on end as to when it's going to lay billowing white blankets over the land.

Fortunately there are some signs that I think are worth looking out for, such as a woolly white circle around the moon. If it is some distance from the moon, that should give plenty of time for the prudent to prepare for a storm.

On the other hand, if the white woolly ring is hugging the moon closely, a snow blizzard is imminent whether you have prepared for it or not.

So it all depends on how much attention you pay to winter weather signs or the prophecies that go along with them. Whether they're right or wrong doesn't really matter that much, as they have probably taken your mind off something that would have been a source of worry.

But there's no doubt about one thing - here in the Highlands, the higher you climb, the more dramatically the temperature changes.

While the Tummel waters are still lapping to the whims of a

westerly wind, a mere mile or two takes me over Kynachan Hill to Kinardochy, a loch lying in the lap of Schiehallion.

It's a different climate altogether up here. There's a sharp sting to every indrawn breath and the surface of this deep, dark little loch is completely frozen over.

Its resident wild birds have left and gone down to the mouths of the burns which are still bubbling cheerfully into the top of Loch Tummel.

There's an abundance of food here for the wild duck and they get it by sticking their tails in the air and guddling in the burn's gravelly bottom that is teeming with minute wildlife.

Meantime, the menfolk of Tummel and Rannoch are hoping that the ice on Loch Kinardochy will soon become strong enough to "hold a horse and cart" and, most importantly, that the snow will stay away and not cover up and spoil the mirror-like surface that was just meant for a curling match.

And, when the ice is just right, there is no thought of further work in any of the menfolk's minds as they flock to Kinardochy, carrying polished curling stones, to compete with each other.

The hills ring with their shouts of exhilaration when the granite stones settle in the proper places, and shudder to the deep groans of despair when they don't.

A hotelier usually turns up around midday with his car groaning under a mountain of meat pies which probably helps to keep him on the road, and a big churn of hot soup that slurps waves of leek and potato over the back seat at every bump and slide in the snow.

He always gets a rapturous welcome from the curlers who stop to partake of his hospitality, while one of the shepherds' collies slips into the car to appreciatively sup up all the spilt soup.

There's romance linked with the loch, too. It concerns the lovely daughter of a local laird who was wilful, went her own way and, in general, was a great trial to her father.

He kept inviting young men from well-known, titled wealthy families, but his wayward daughter would have nothing to do with them.

44

A young French aristocrat, and a skilled swordsman, hoping to attract the daughter's attention, challenged an English nobleman to a duel. They fought for her favours under a full moon on the ice of Loch Kinardochy.

The Sassenach was, himself, a champion with the rapier so the two of them, wounded and utterly exhausted after an epic battle, were both glad to agree that honour had been seen to be satisfied.

The daughter, an excited spectator of the fight, disappeared during the hand-shaking.

She had an assignation with a handsome young shepherd she had first met while walking her spaniel on the hills. Thereafter they had secret meetings.

Sometimes he brought his pair of Highland ponies and, riding them bareback, they flew over the moor as free as the air itself.

But her father found out and was furious. He forbade her ever to see the young man again, but they still had idyllic clandestine meetings.

He would whistle in the darkness like a wild bird, under her window, and she would escape, tiptoeing out into the night, to share her heart with his on the heathery banks of Loch Kinardochy.

Finally, the father, in desperation, sent his daughter to stay with a friend in Spain. He at least knew his only child's love of horses, and his friend had stables full of fine animals that were renowned all over the world.

The young shepherd never saw her again. He couldn't stay in the same surroundings without her, so he set out to start a new life in Australia.

It's so quiet at Kinardochy tonight and the sky at the darkening is a luminous, duck-egg blue. A flock of widgeon have just flown in with muffled wingbeats.

It matters not to them that the loch is frozen over, for they are hardy little birds, well used to Icelandic weather.

Like geese, they are grazers and have come here for the sweet, spiky green grass that grows between the bunches of heather.

The drakes are beautiful birds, their plumage blending blush-pink with powder-blue, and they wear a distinctive band of cream as a headdress.

As if afraid of losing touch, the widgeon call to each other continuously with a sweet, lilting, intimate whistle.

I only have to close my eyes and it becomes the soft, secretive sound of the young shepherd telling his sweetheart that he is there still - waiting to hold her in his arms.

Rory My Friend Of The Air

*Every time I see a raven flying bold and free, I wonder if it's
Rory - and if he remembers when he was one of our family.*

Spring comes slowly to the Highlands, especially when the
March winds blow in from the North-East. Blinding blizzards of
snow can smother the snowdrops and send the multi-coloured
crocuses cowering back into their bulbs.

The peeking primroses cover their faces with their green frond-
like hands, while the daffodils, not easily deceived and always
fearful of March and April, steadfastly refuse to open their buds
until assured of a long, loving kiss from the sun.

The birds take a different view, especially the missel thrush. He
isn't called the "storm cock" for nothing, as he sings defiantly into
the teeth of the blizzard. His message, to all the other birds, is that
the time has come to find a mate, make a home, and rear a family.

The ravens were the first to answer his call, circling the peak of
Creag Mhor to claim this nesting place as their own. They didn't
even have to take the trouble to make a nest. There was an eyrie
there, built by a paid of golden eagles and deserted.

This was a bonus for the ravens who only had to weave a blanket
of sheep's wool through the frame of carefully-constructed silver
birch boughs.

All went smoothly with the ravens' romance until one morning
in May. The peace of the Creag Mhor peak was shattered with their
raucous croaks as they took turns to battle with a big buzzard that
flew overhead.

The buzzard had only one thing in mind. It lowered its head and
looked down its cruel, curved beak to gaze, with glowing golden

eyes, at the young raven that had tumbled out of the nest and now lay sprawled on a ledge far below.

As I watched, the buzzard brushed aside the ravens' aerial attack and flexed its talons. Any moment now it would dive down and pick up the young bird.

Yelling at the top of my voice, I raced towards the rocks and clawed my way up the cliff face. The buzzard uttered a shrieking, cat-like mew and with a wave of its massive wingspan, veered away.

I reached the young raven. Having stuffed the squawking bundle of black feathers into my game bag, I made a perilous attempt to climb the rest of the way to the ravens' nest. But there was no way I could surmount or circumvent its craggy overhang of rock, which appeared specially designed to prevent predators from approaching the nest.

The buzzard had gone now. Should I leave the young one on the ledge I had reached? The parent birds circled above me like two black brushes painting their anxiety in the sky.

I knew they would feed and care for the young raven but it would not have the safety and security of the nest. The buzzard would return, or a wild cat or a fox.

Then my mind was made up for me. The young raven in the nest peeped over the edge and let out a penetrating scream which was answered from my bag with a muffled croak. The parents, in a meaningful dive, almost swept me from my perch.

That settled it, I retired as hastily as I could and the young raven, christened Rory, was installed in the stable at Croft Douglas.

Feeding him was quite a problem at first. He totally ignored the tasty pieces of chopped liver I placed temptingly in front of him. I tried prising open his beak to slip in a piece of meat but to no avail. Rory just spat it out and sat back, blinking stupidly.

Next, I tried the natural approach and treated him to some full-blooded, deep-throated croaks. Rory's reactions were immediate! He jumped up and down, screeching excitedly, and I found myself staring down his ample gullet. Quickly I popped a piece of liver in.

I repeated this procedure half a dozen times, then at last, Rory squatted down on the manger, blinking contentedly.

The young raven grew rapidly and had a finger, or rather a feather, in everything that went on around Croft Douglas. He supervised the feeding of the hens and the milking of the house cow and would try to beat the cat in a wild race for the saucerful of milk. It was usually a dead heat and they sipped, one on either side, and swore at each other.

Rory was a fantastic mimic. He would mew softly and call the kittens - then chuckle in delight at their bewilderment. He could cluck with the laying hens, copy the crowing of the cock and bark like a dog.

I felt sure that, with a little coaxing, I could get him to talk, so each time I fed him I said slowly. "Rory likes liver".

One morning, Rory looked straight at me over his empty plate and in growly voice, drawn deep down from his breast feathers, said, "Rory likes liver".

Tarra, the collie, and Rory became great friends. Together they herded everything - chickens, kittens and ducklings. But when Tarra was called upon to round up some sheep, Rory was hard put to it to keep up and hopped, flapped, and croaked in despair, until forced to spread his wings.

To his own and Tarra's astonishment, he floated effortlessly. From that moment he directed all proceedings from the air.

The hens weren't giving their usual supply of eggs. I wondered why, until I spotted Rory shuffling stealthily into the henhouse. I peeped around the door and saw Rory crooning huskily to a setting hen. He tenderly tickled her breast feathers with the point of his beak, then robbed her of the newly-laid eggs.

Using his wings for acceleration, he flapped out of the henhouse, triumphantly carrying his trophy. His surprise at seeing me had to be seen to be believed. He sat back on his tail, hiding his head, and the egg, under his wing!

But Rory fully repaid his egg debt when a dog weasel crept into the farmyard.

A mother hen spotted his stealthy approach and shrieked an alarm call. All her brood immediately sought the shelter of her feathered breast as she prepared to defend herself and her chicks.

Help came from the air. Rory, dropping like a stone, dealt the weasel a stunning blow with his beak, picked him up in his claws and made a laboured take-off.

The weasel recovered consciousness in mid-air and squirming around in Rory's claws, bit him savagely in the chest. Rory squawked in pain, released his grip and the weasel dropped down with a thump on the turf, to slink painfully away.

But Rory was badly wounded. He didn't eat a bite for two days. I feared his wounds were infected so I bathed them with whisky and put a little into some warm milk for him to sip.

He swallowed, blinked rapidly, then whispered hoarsely, "Rory likes liver", and proved it by disposing of a saucerful.

Within a week, Rory was back to his old self. Then the wanderlust claimed him as he foraged further and further afield.

One day when I saw Rory rise replete from a rabbit carcase he had found, I knew he had acquired the priceless gift of independence.

I tucked him under my arm, marvelling at how much he had grown since we had first met, and set off for Creag Mhor, right back to the old eyrie and nesting place.

I held Rory tightly in my arms as my fingers fondly stroked his every feather into its proper place. I realised how much I loved him and his funny ways. I had to blink repeatedly to clear the mist from my eyes, but Rory was looking at, and outblinking me.

I threw him high in the sky. As he circled and inspected the nest, I quickly disappeared lest he be tempted to follow me back to the croft.

A week later I climbed the Creag again and stopped, when I was only halfway up, to watch a kestrel hawk hovering delicately above me. Suddenly, it screamed and dived straight down the cliff face, fleeing from the black shape that was hurtling towards me. It was Rory!

He landed a few feet from me, dancing around with delight. With a swoop of his great wings, he rose and circled round and round my head, croaking his pleasure at our meeting. I didn't trust myself to croak back, or linger, and so possibly weaken the links that now bound him to the wild.

As he tilted a wing to show off his latest flying manoeuvre, I waved a fond farewell and raced away.

Every March, when the ravens return to Creag Mhor to inspect and to tidy up their nesting site they treat us to a great display of aerobatics. There is a large cock bird who can outfly them all and execute perfectly the ravens' speciality, sweeping down in a perfect dive, pulling out to level up, then fold his wings to leisurely roll over.

I like to think this is Rory.

A Boy's Own Story

Boarding school was to teach me many, many lessons - and
some of the hardest never appeared in schoolbooks or on
the blackboard...

The son of a big-business father and an ambitious, career-minded mother, I was packed off, with my name-taped clothing, to boarding school at a tender age.

After the first week I learned not to cry in public but to save my sobs for the darkness of night, when I could stifle them in my pillow. How I loathed all the restrictions and regimentation, particularly in the evening when, with the song thrush still singing to the setting sun, the Silence Bell demanded that we accept the close of day.

Sleep did not come easily and I found solace in writing down the thoughts that came straight from my heart. I got so absorbed that, when darkness came, I still continued to write by torchlight under the bedclothes.

I wrote about everything, including a little frog I had found in a corner of the tennis courts. As I smuggled it into my dormitory, I told myself I had only to kiss her and she would turn into a handsome princess.

But I hesitated, not that I minded kissing a frog. I felt I couldn't take the risk that it might all go wrong and my dream would be destroyed.

So I stayed with my dream and, when no-one was looking, slipped the little frog under an attractive piece of shrubbery, assuring her we would meet again when I was a little older.

My bed, strictly against rules, became the most popular

rendezvous after the evening bell. It groaned under the weight of the other boys heaped all over it as they read my stories.

I sat back on my pillow and studied all the faces. The expressions ranged from sheer astonishment and open-mouthed amazement to fits of giggling. For the first time since starting school, I felt the weight of loneliness being lifted from me. I had made all those friends through my writing.

We weren't allowed pets at school, but the headmaster had a big, black cat. I thought this most unfair until the opportunity to own a small pet, that no-one would notice, came my way.

The gardener had a house in the school grounds and his daughter had a pet mouse with a family of six cuddly, chocolate-coloured babies. The light of envy must have glittered in my eyes because this kind, unselfish little girl gave me one!

I was ecstatic and kept it in a shoe-box in the bottom of my wardrobe, letting it out at night to exercise by racing up and down between the sheets. My friends ringed around my bed, the corners of the sheets stuffed in their mouths to stifle the squeals of delight at the little mouse's acrobatic antics.

I took some water from my carafe and liberally sprinkled my little mouse and solemnly christened him "Squiggles". Oh, the hours of after-lights-out fun we had with him!

A nosey housemaid spoiled it all. She had, in curiosity, lifted the box lid and Squiggles sat up and begged to be lifted out. The housemaid's terrified shrieks easily beat the fire alarm for volume.

Authority, however, was not amused. The gardener was sent for to take Squiggles away and I was confined to the dormitory for a day on bread and water. I didn't mind that. I had broken the school rules, but how my heart ached over losing my little friend.

I finally found comfort in my pen, writing reams about Squiggles and how much I missed him.

My pile of writing was growing to an embarrassing size and I was glad when my father called to see me and I could take it from its hiding place under my shoes and give it to him, before it was discovered.

He spent some time analysing my efforts. Then he told me I might just make a writer and that he would pay me a pound for each one of my articles that was returned with a rejection slip, until I had one accepted.

This was just the encouragement I needed. From that moment my burning ambition was to be a best-selling author. My financial figuring told me that, with the "Editor regrets" arrangement, I couldn't lose.

Out of the school grounds we always walked in crocodile formation. It was so boring. But, on one occasion, we were taken as a special treat to see a matinee of "Beau Geste". On the walk back to school, I became, in my mind, a legionnaire marching in line across the desert, my boots sinking in the sand, every step a tortured move towards the fort.

When we reached school, I was exhausted with the desert march I had conjured up in my mind. For once, I laid my head on the pillow, thankful for Lights Out and the Silence Bell.

But, in my sleep, it started all over again, and we eventually reached the gaunt, grey, stone building in the middle of nowhere.

We had just started our meal of bully beef and biscuits when the bugle sounded "Battle Stations". We all positioned ourselves at a slot in the wall and fired at the milling mob of dusky warriors attacking us until our rifles were red hot.

My friends fell and the brutal sergeant propped their bodies up against the slots and stuck rifles in their limp hands. As I watched, he roared at me, "Keep firing!"

I knew I had seen his face before. It was the headmaster!

The enemy hordes swarmed up the walls, standing on each other's shoulders, and I found myself almost rubbing noses with a black face, its eyes glinting evilly.

My shrieks wakened the entire dormitory and I found myself gazing through the bars at the end of my bed at the dusky face of the headmaster's cat.

Baxter was the biggest boy in the dormitory and a merciless

bully. He seemed to resent the way I made friends with the other boys and specialised in surreptitiously rumpling up our wardrobes just before inspection.

We knew who had done it, but didn't tell tales and took the punishment without a word.

One morning my wardrobe was found full of apples. I protested, to no avail, that I had no idea where they had come from, knowing full well that Baxter was behind this and I could never tell and so lose the respect of the other boys.

What really hurt more than the caning was being made to return the apples to the school gardener and apologise.

That night I wrote a story about a man, imprisoned unjustly, who made friends with a mouse. He fed it scraps from his meagre meals and, in return, the mouse taught him to believe in himself, and win his way, against all odds, to freedom. I couldn't see the paper as I penned the last words.

About this time I had accumulated 25 slips of paper, saying, "The Editor regrets". Wealth and my writing seemed to be marching hand in hand, until I sent this one about the man and the mouse to a nationwide magazine and received a nice letter back from the editor and a cheque for five pounds!

A month later the headmaster called me out at Assembly, waving a copy of the magazine above his head.

"Many of you here", he said, "will have distinguished careers, but here we have a boy who has already proved himself as a writer".

He patted me on the head and, putting his hand in his pocket, presented me with two half crowns.

Baxter was waiting for me in the washroom during the lunch break.

"Who's the clever boy, then"? he said, bringing his hands together to slap me smartly on both cheeks. With my face stinging I swung wildly at him.

This was just what Baxter wanted. They didn't nickname him "Basher" for nothing. He rammed his fist into my face. I landed up hanging over a wash-hand basin watching a scarlet stream blending with the rushing tap water.

That night I wrote about a boy's battle against tremendous odds. As he fell he heard a voice saying, "He wins who rises one more time".

My next meeting with my oppressor was on the rugby field. Baxter was the captain of the school team and I had been chosen as one of the "rest" for a practice game before an important match.

It was in the first five minutes that I found myself the only one left between Baxter and the scoring line. He tanked towards me with the ball tucked under his arm, puffing like an express train.

I felt to wait and be run over would be fatal, so I sprinted to meet him. My head hit his stomach like a battering ram and my arms locked themselves around his legs. Together, we tumbled over and over, then lay still.

I awoke in the hospital with my head cradled on the breast of a motherly matron. I could have lain there for ever.

"There, there, lad", she said gently, stroking my aching brow. "Just a bit of concussion but you're all right now. You can go whenever you feel like it. You came off better than the big lad. He's got two broken ribs and a badly-bruised tummy".

I dressed quickly, selected a large apple from the bowl of fruit by my bedside and went across to the other bed. How on earth, I wondered, was I ever afraid of this fellow. He looked such a poor, pathetic heap, lying wordlessly under the blankets as I presented him with the apple.

"Sorry about the ribs, old chap", I said airily as I turned to go.

I am still writing, but rejection slips no longer assure me of financial gain. I am now fearful of receiving one. I have learned to regard, with respect, the little note that says, "The Editor regrets..."

The Protection of Melanie

*From the brightness of her eye and the trust in her heart, I
knew, from the moment I helped her out of the egg, that this
little hen pheasant and I were going to be very special
friends...*

Her Ladyship surveyed me from head to toe through her
lorgnette and then told me, in a concise but friendly tone that,
despite my lack of experience, I had been selected from numerous
applicants because she liked my handwriting. She was pleased to
appoint me as her gamekeeper.

Since I was a small boy I had always wanted to be a gamekeeper
and now, at 17, this was my big chance.

I started work in the rearing field. The stock of pheasants
needed a big boost in numbers and this was the place to do it. I filled
the rows of wooden boxes with "broody hens" brought from the
surrounding farms, and from the dozens of pheasants' eggs bought
in to provide new blood and strong, vigorous birds, I gave each of
the hens 15 eggs to sit on.

Their reward for the patience they showed came on hatching
day.

Excitement ran like an electric current through the nesting
boxes as the foster-mothers rose carefully to give air to the
hatching chickens. All except a little speckled hen who sat on
hopefully.

I examined her eggs carefully. They were all infertile, except
one. I held it to my ear and could hear the rustle of life: a frantic
"peeping" and a desperate tap-tapping on the shell, like an SOS for
help. And no wonder - there was a thick band of shell around the

middle of the egg that the chick could never hope to penetrate. Gently, I chipped the eggshell.

As if it sensed the moment of release, the chick, with a supreme effort, heaved off the top of the egg and ended up - a tiny, warm, pulsating piece of flesh and feather - in the palm of my hand.

Later that day, I looked into the speckled hen's nest box. A fluffy, bronze and black head with tiny beady eyes peeped back at me from underneath a curtain of speckled feathers.

In no time at all the chicks grew their first feathers; the cock birds' plumage showing the first splashes of brilliant colouring, whilst the hens were clad in soft, sombre shades of brown - a clever camouflage designed to protect the future mother birds.

But my chick was different. Her feathers were a rich chestnut, burnished with copper bordered in black, and tipped delicately with a fringe of gold.

I had never seen such a beautiful bird and I named her Melanie.

The young pheasants were soon ready to be moved to the coverts - lines of silver spruce and larch trees that would be their future home. Every day I visited them, my game-bag bulging with boiled maize.

Melanie always stood aloof as the others gobbled the grain, knowing that she could eat at leisure from my hand.

In my heart of hearts, though, I knew it was wrong to make Melanie a pet, especially when I was introducing her, together with all the other young pheasants, to a precarious way of life in the wilds.

One night when the moon was full, I had to watch over my charges. I struggled in vain against sleep when suddenly, a shot rang out.

I was wide awake when the next shot exploded just above my head. I saw a flame from a gun muzzle, and the sharp smell of cordite filled my nostrils. I saw something else, too, a shadowy figure almost on top of me.

In a rugby tackle I dived at his legs and the poacher fell, striking his head against a larch tree.

I picked up his gun and the dead pheasants. Whilst I grieved over each one, I was glad that Melanie was not among them.

After this, Melanie decided that the estate coverts were too dangerous and flew out to the farm fields beyond the estate walls. But she found there was danger there, too. One day I saw her picking the elderberries from a tree at the top of the Cruggleton Cliffs.

Someone else saw her - a peregrine falcon hanging high in the sky. And, as Melanie continued to devour the delicious berries, the peregrine folded its wings and descended in a deadly dive.

Fortunately for her, though, this peregrine had once been a trained bird and was still wearing a bell. She heard him and side-slipped as he plunged into the elderberry tree.

With a specially-prepared bait, I trapped the peregrine. He was terribly thin, so I removed the tinkling bell that had betrayed him and been the cause of his starvation. I sent him miles away from Melanie to Kirkcowan Moor where he would be free and welcomed by the keeper who really cared about wildlife.

One of my tasks was to seek out the cunningly-concealed partridge nests and check them daily to ensure they came to no harm.

One morning, I found Melanie sitting on a nest.

Gently, I stroked her breast feathers and she rose a little to show me the secret she was cradling so closely: 10 beautiful brown and olive-tinted eggs.

The glint that sparkled from her eye was full of the confidence that I was a friend, and eventually the day came when Melanie really did need me.

She was still sitting on the nest, but the ferns that helped conceal it were spattered with blood and I could see that some of her flight feathers were missing. She looked straight at me, desperately pleading for help.

I brushed the back of my hand under her breast and discovered there were only three eggs left. I had been on my way home, tired and hungry, but now I sat down by Melanie's side. We would see this thing out together.

Some time later the still of the approaching night was shattered by horrendous sounds of snuffling, snorting and squealing as two giant hedgehogs shuffled towards Melanie. They were back to battle with the brave hen pheasant and try to take the rest of her eggs. They were robbers who were quite capable of killing, too.

I bundled them both into my game-bag and took them back with me to the estate garden where, within its walls, they could spend their time atoning for their wickedness by living on the pests that attacked the vegetables.

Three days later Melanie's nest contained only eggshells. The three chicks had hatched. Hen pheasants are usually not the best of mothers but Melanie seemed determined not to lose any of her precious babies. If one got stuck in a ditch she would run back to give encouraging clucks until it made a supreme effort to join her and the brood.

One October morning I received a message from Charles, the footman, that Her Ladyship's son, the "Honourable", and his sporting guests would like a day's shooting over the Cruggleton Farm.

This was part of my job that I never got used to, or cared for.

We walked the stubble fields where the partridges were feeding. They fled at our approach but the shooting line moved forward mercilessly.

Suddenly, I was horrified to see Melanie's head pop out of the turnip leaves right in the middle of the advancing shooting line. I tried to shout, "Don't shoot", but the words were strangled in my throat. In desperation, I clutched my neck and found the Command Whistle, which only I was allowed to wear.

I blew a short, sharp blast and, as if by magic, the line halted. Even the gundogs, with front paws raised, stood stock still. All, except the "Honourable".

He walked towards me, tall and forbidding, and towered over me with raised eyebrows. I had planned to plead for my pheasant but, instead, found myself saying, stiffly:

"There are special birds ahead. We need them for stock".

The "Honourable" never questioned my authority and, in a loud clear voice said, "Pass the message. No shooting until the next whistle".

I waved the line forward. Two young pheasant hens rose together, the picture of their mother, then a velvety-black, young cock pheasant with a scarlet headdress and plumage patterned with green and gold and, last of all, Melanie herself. Her flight was unhurried and majestic.

I felt that the glance back over her wing was for me and knew I could never let Melanie down. She had taught me what beauty and bravery were all about, that the bonds of real friendship were unbreakable and, above all, that trust between two living creatures was something sacred, never to be betrayed.

The Gift To See

Wendy was a mother-in-law with a difference. Not only did
she have second sight - but she believed she owed her gift
to a certain ancient brooch...

Wendy had the "second sight", recognised in the Highlands as
a gift granted to only a chosen few, bringing with it the ability to
"see" an event before it has happened.

Her daughter, Irralee, a tousled-haired, tilted-nosed, freckle-
faced girl, in her early teens, with whom I wasn't even on speaking
terms, had told my mother boldly that, one day, she would marry
me. She qualified her statement confidently by saying, "Wendy
has seen the wedding and says it will be blessed by birdsong".

This caused a great amount of hilarity in my family, but 10
years later, Irralee and I were married in the parish manse, whilst
a choir of chaffinches sang their hearts out in the gardens!

In the years that followed, I learned to live with Wendy's
visions, or at least try to come to terms with them. But something
inside me never forgot to be fearful of opening her letters. The
contents of these would run for page after page, pointing out the
pitfalls that lay ahead of me, ending with a postscript and possible
plans to avoid them.

Then there were the telegrams that were guaranteed to send
shock waves through my entire system. These would spell out in
short, staccato sentences, paths and people to be avoided.

But most frightening of all was the sudden, insistent shrieking
of the telephone in the middle of the night. These calls would tear
me away from a blissful sleep to listen, half consciously, to a voice
that spoke with the patience of someone addressing a child, with

a warning that a journey planned for the next day must, under no circumstances, be undertaken.

Wendy's visions were not confined to the family alone. Deeply religious, she never lost a chance to worship, in church or out of it.

One Sunday morning, in the Barclay Church in Edinburgh, just when the minister was leading his congregation into a spirited rendering of "Rock Of Ages", Wendy rose from her seat, sprinted up the aisle and shook the shoulder of a man seated at the end of a pew.

"You are wanted urgently at home". She gasped and, grasping his hand, dragged him to the door and out into the street. Together, they took a taxi back to his house where they found his wife had fainted and fallen into the fireplace, her face only inches from the flames.

Another time, at the harbour at Berwick-upon-Tweed, Wendy spoke to a trawlerman, just as he was about to board his ship.

"Why", she asked, "is there a black flag flying at the mast?"

"Lady", the trawlerman replied respectfully, "there is no flag there".

"Oh, yes there is," Wendy insisted, "and it's flying in mourning for those who sail in her".

The seaman was from the Islands and had been brought up to believe in the "second sight". The boat sailed without him, and never returned.

When Wendy was visiting Harris, she apologised to her hostess for arriving at a time of mourning, only to be assured that there had been no deaths in the area for the past five years.

"But", Wendy said, "I saw a funeral procession with six men carrying a coffin down the winding path from the big white house on the hill".

Her hostess told her laughingly that the man living in the white house was very healthy and an eligible bachelor on whom more than one local girl had set her sights.

Some time later, she wrote to Wendy with the news that the young man had, indeed, died and events had been just as she had said.

What disturbed me most was my mother-in-law's total confidence that her visions would materialise, the fact that she was always right, and never said, "I told you so".

Wendy was also a Nationalist with a capital "N", and wanted to tell the world about her beliefs. She found the perfect place for free speech at The Mound, in Edinburgh, on Sunday nights.

To say she was carried away by her oratory was literally true, by the police! After a night in a cold police cell, Wendy was charged with the crime of sedition.

To our relief, the charge was dropped and Wendy was released. Apparently, authority was glad to see her go as she had spent her time drawing caricatures of the Police Chief and city dignitaries on the walls of her cell, with an indelible pencil!

Irralee, like her mother, had ideas of her own and insisted on having her baby at home. Wendy came to admire her new granddaughter and lend a helping hand.

One dark night, when the day's work was done, and Irralee was asleep with her little one, Wendy and I sat, one on either side of the fireplace. She sat with her knitting needles flying and it came to me that this could be the moment to ask Wendy why, at the pinnacle of her life as a writer, painter, broadcaster and television personality, she continued to fight so fiercely for Scotland.

Wendy put down her knitting, picked up the poker and made a sword-like thrust at a blazing birch log in the fire, sending sparks flying in formation up the chimney.

With the poker still held firmly in her hand, she told me that her mother had left her a plaidie brooch with a note, saying it had been worn by a clansman in battle and her last wish was that it should always be kept as a family heirloom.

Wendy paused for a moment, I knew she had more to tell and waited patiently.

"The brooch is a huge square-cut crystal, set in a circle of solid silver", Wendy went on, "and I only wear it on special occasions, but always keep it on my bedside table.

"One night I was awakened by a brilliant blue light flashing from the crystal. I looked into its centre and saw a picture of an old well, so real that when I reached out to touch it, I felt my fingers sink into the clammy, cold dampness of the green moss surrounding its circular sides.

"There was no more sleep for me that night, and in the dawn's early light I pinned the plaidie brooch to my shoulder and set off for Culloden Moor. As if my footsteps were guided to it, I found the well and, exhausted, lay down and gazed into the cold, clear water, at the pattern of pebbles that covered its bottom. It wasn't a deep well but was fed and kept fresh by an underground spring.

"Mirrored in its water I saw the plaidie brooch with every facet of its crystal flashing. I then found myself looking into my own reflection. There was red blood dripping down into my eyes and I felt a throbbing, blinding, unbearable pain in my forehead and tasted the saltiness of the scarlet stream as it seeped down into my mouth, and left me with a raging thirst.

"With cupped hands I drank deeply from the waters of the well, and rose, convinced that I had been here before in battle, and now must fight again for Scotland".

Wendy brushed the back of her hand across her forehead. She always wore a long, attractive fringe and I waited with bated breath to see if a scar lay underneath. But the curtain of hair rose only a fraction before settling back into place.

Wendy left the plaidie brooch to me when she died, with a note saying that the crystal would show a picture of the Scottish Assembly opening ceremony in Edinburgh, before it took place.

She was never wrong, so I watch the plaidie brooch and wait...

The Goddle - A Wild Goose That Came To Stay

She was born to a wild goose and fostered by a hen, but there was only one person The Goddle really belonged to - the crofter who had given her the chance of life.

It was last spring that I found The Goddle. Or rather, The Goddle found me.

I was wandering along the lochside, marvelling that, after the hardest winter I had ever known, the earth had somehow recovered and was busy breathing life into everything that had rooted in her. The silver birch seemed to have "dressed up" almost overnight, countless primrose plants had opened their green fingers to display handfuls of dainty yellow flowers and, running through them towards me, with its head and neck outstretched, was a tiny gosling, crying piteously.

As I stroked its soft downy body it uttered a series of ecstatic "whee-whee-whees" at finding someone to belong to. It cocked its head to one side and, with a bright liquid eye, looked at me trustingly.

I sat the little one in the crook of my arm and, looking around for its mother, found only the nest, cunningly concealed under a juniper bush. There only remained the lining of grass and bracken filled with hatched eggshells.

The gosling looked to be only two or three days old and I guessed the rest of the brood must be somewhere near. Looking out across the water, I spotted the wild mother goose with her little ones bobbing, like a train of corks, behind her.

I put the gosling down at the water's edge, stepped back behind a tree and left it alone. Once again, it started its plaintive cries but, if the mother heard it, she didn't look back. The gosling turned to me, deciding, with a series of "whee-whees", that I was the only one who could possibly help, and settled, once more with a "whee" of relief, in the crook of my arm.

So, I turned for home, reflecting that the gosling's mother must be one of the few wild geese that didn't return to their homeland at the approach of spring, but elected to rear their families in the Highlands of Scotland.

When I reached Croft Douglas, Irralee was at the door. Anything to do with animals or birds gets her immediate and undivided attention and the mundane everyday household chores, which she finds so difficult to come to terms with, are abandoned gleefully on occasions such as this.

The little one was further comforted, assured that its future happiness was our main concern, put in a box lined with hay, and placed on top of the hot-water tank while we had a cup of tea and debated what was best to do.

"There's Turnip Shed", I said. This was a hen who had earned her name by always choosing to lay in the building set aside for the sole purpose of storing the winter's supply of succulent swede turnips.

This year she had laid a clutch of eggs in one of the shed's most secluded corners and, only the day before yesterday, had hatched out 10 downy chicks.

But something else had thought the chicks plump and attractive. A dog weasel had found a way in to the turnip shed and in the time it took me to snatch up and load my gun there was only one chick left and Turnip Shed, who had fought so bravely, was shielding her last chicken with her head bowed and bloody.

Irralee bathed Turnip Shed's wounds, put salve on her torn ear lobes and left her to croon, brokenly, over her last chicken.

This was the answer! We would give Turnip Shed the gosling to help replace the rest of her brood.

She never gave a murmur as I slipped the gosling under her breast feathers. I supposed that she had gone through so much that any situation, for the time being, found her with the feeling that she just couldn't care less. So the gosling settled in gratefully and warmed its back on Turnip Shed's breast, shoulder to shoulder with the last little black and yellow chicken.

We had agreed that we would not name the gosling, as it was a wild one, but gradually, because of its air of independence, we referred to it as The Goddle. It appeared to acknowledge that its foster mother provided warmth when it was most needed, but that was all and, as the stubs of its first feathers sprouted, independence became absolute, and The Goddle spent all its spare time seeking me out in a determined effort to establish our relationship more firmly.

In no time at all, the gosling was eating out of my hand, daintily pecking the wheat from my palm and, when the grain was finished, gently chiddling the skin on my hand with the tip of its beak, making it abundantly clear that, in its opinion, we belonged to one another.

Turnip Shed tried desperately to win her foster child back, first by a series of persistent, persuasive clucks and, when that failed, produced her trump card - a fat, wriggling worm tugged forcibly from its earth home and deposited in front of The Goddle which, knowing the gift was presented as something special and not wishing to offend, picked it up.

The hen clucked her approval, but The Goddle plainly regarded the worm as a really revolting object and just didn't know what to do next.

In the meantime, the worm had escaped from the other side of The Goddle's beak. Being an intelligent bird, it pretended to have swallowed it, just to please its foster mother.

Hay time found The Goddle fully feathered in delicately-pencilled blue and grey with chestnut overtones edged with cream. I decided, then, that she was feminine, not only because of her neat, trim figure, but because of her way of turning her head on one side.

She also talked a lot!

The Goddle wasted no time in trying out her fully-feathered wings. She had no-one to give her flying lessons and did everything by trial and error. In the beginning, her awkward, flapping take-offs and bumpy, bouncing landings were something to make me close my eyes and shudder.

But, as time went by, The Goddle's determined efforts to fly achieved perfection and she showed off shamelessly, gliding over the roof-tops of the house and outbuildings, then turning gracefully in mid-air to launch herself straight at me, only to lift a wing at the last moment, leaving me ruffled, but unscathed.

The cockerel, a majestic Maran holding the title of The Magnificent Brute, had mixed feelings about The Goddle. He knew she was not of his kind but, nevertheless, held her in deep respect, especially when the foxes came down from the forestry plantations, creeping softly and silently through the undergrowth to make a daring, daylight raid.

But no matter how close they hugged their bellies to the ground, the vigilant Goddle always spotted them and, with head pointed to the heavens, trumpeted the alarm call. Since her self-appointed duty as sentinel, the losses in the flock had ceased dramatically.

But The Magnificent Brute brooded. He either didn't approve, or was jealous of The Goddle's status with the hens. One morning when I was hand feeding her, he launched a furious attack behind my back and sank his spurs in my bare arm.

Before I had recovered, the outraged Goddle went into action. With wings half open and her head and neck in one straight line, she launched herself at the cockerel. The cockerel let out an astonished croak, turned tail, and fled.

He always kept the hens confined to the farm steading when The Goddle went for a walk with me to the lochside.

When the waters of the loch came in sight, The Goddle would spread her wings and land with a resounding smack and a glorious splash in the sheltered waters of the bay. This was her paradise.

Winter came, and with it came wild geese by the hundreds,

searching for an easier way of life than their Scandinavian homeland afforded at this time.

The Goddle heard them coming and, as her excitement mounted, she ran around on pink tiptoes like a feathered ballerina, with wings half open and her head pointing to the sky, answering the call of the wild ones. The incoming geese heard her and dipped over the croft.

I watched and waited. I had a few anxious moments when The Goddle took to the air. Was she going to join the wild ones? She contented herself by flying in wide circles around the croft.

Christmas came and, with it, heavy snowfalls. The Goddle rejoiced in this new white world and complained loudly when the hens, after testing the depth of the snow with tentative feet, retired to the comfort of their house and refused to join her. So she developed a winter carnival all for herself, with vertical take-offs and long, breathtaking skiing touch-downs on the steep slopes that invariably ended with crash landings in a snow drift.

The Highland cattle hadn't been besporting themselves in the snow. They had been too busy looking for something to eat and reported back home, bellowing that their search had all been in vain.

The Goddle, always interested in what was going on, followed me as I spread out some hay for them. She studied the snow buntings as they flitted around the hairy Highlanders, picking up the grass seeds that fell with every mouthful. She also looked long and hard at me when I gently scratched Drumbuie, the big bull, where he liked it best, between his broad shoulder blades.

At this point The Goddle showed that she, too, was not immune to the sting of jealousy and expressed her total disapproval with a session of honking.

That winter was harsh, and one afternoon, during a lull in a storm, the hens ventured to leave their house and, like the sheep, became trapped. They managed to reach a sheltered spot in the cattle pens and were surrounded by a deep drift of snow.

There was one thing The Goddle hated and that was to be left alone, so she sought me out and, with repeated clarion calls, led me away. I followed her and together we found the hens. One wrong move, and they would scatter.

I wasn't sure what to do, but The Goddle was. She breasted her way through the drift, had a "word" with the cockerel, then made her way out again, like a feathered tank.

The cockerel followed, leading his flock step by step through the buffeting blizzard until the henhouse was reached. At this point, The Goddle stood aside and was the last to go in. I put the question into the darkness of the henhouse, the one I always asked when "shutting in".

"Are you all right"? And got the Goddle's reassuring, "Whee-whee-whee".

The days grew longer, the wild geese became aware of it and the sky was filled with their arrow-headed formations, all pointing in the same direction. They were going home.

The Goddle was beside herself with an excitement that grew to fever pitch. I and my handful of golden kibbled maize were totally ignored; she heard only the call of the wild ones. The air was alive with their wing beats.

The Goddle didn't even have a last look round or say, "Goodbye". I watched her join the tail of the last formation and vanish from sight.

Friendship can only be measured at the time of parting. The Goddle had gone!

I was full of misgivings. Would her wings be strong enough to cross the North Sea? And, worse still, I had taught her to trust mankind - she would be the first to fall to the hunter's gun.

Irralee came looking for me.

"Tea's ready", she said, and added, "Have you been crying?"

"No", I replied gruffly. "I've got something in my eyes".

We ate the evening meal in silence. What was there to say? I excused myself. It was time to "shut in". I felt it just would not be the same. Tonight there would be no answering "Whee-whee-whee", when I asked, "Are you all right"?

I turned to have a last look at the darkening sky. There was a spot in the East that, all the time, seemed to get bigger and bigger. I watched it, fascinated, until my ears drummed with a whistling, screaming rush of air, and I was struck with an almighty thump on the chest that sent me flat on my back.

As I lay on the ground my pet goose spread her wings over and around me, nibbling the lobe of my ear, gently chiddling up the track of the salt stain on my cheek.

The Goddle had come back to Croft Douglas and to me.

My Lady Of The Loch

*It dawned like any other day for me but my meeting with one
very beautiful lady was to make it a special one I would
never forget...*

No matter how stealthily the dawn creeps up Loch Tummel, our
cockerel is the first to sense it. He rises from his roosting perch to
slap his wings with a thunderous clap before crowing an almighty
crow that arouses his slumbering wives to join him in a cackling
chorus.

Over the breakfast table, my wife and I planned out the rest of
the day. First, I must check our herd of Highland cattle. They were
nowhere to be seen in the fields nearby.

As I set out to search for them, Irralee called after me, "Take
Misty with you. She needs a walk".

Misty is our daughter Shona's dog. A Keeshond, she revels in
an unrivalled reputation as a guard dog and woe betide anyone, or
anything, that comes between her and what she is "minding".

Misty also has a jaw like a bear trap. I know, having felt the snap
of it when attempting to rescue somebody who had stepped out of
line to her way of thinking! Both Shona and Irralee assured me that
the dog didn't mean it and that I, unfortunately, had just got in the
way.

So far, that day, apart from almost giving Danny, the postman,
a heart attack, Misty had not put a paw wrong. As we wound our
way through the woods, she shared my interest in a ring of pigeon's
feathers that marked the spot where a hawk had made his kill, and
the cool, clear pool of spring water whose moist, soft, sandy edge
told of the sly fox, a bustling badger and the dainty roe deer that

had paused to sip.

The hazel trees were bedecked with newly-formed nuts and the silver birches reached down to run their fingers through my hair. We finally found the cattle munching their way through a tasty stretch of lochside pasture. The bull blew disdainfully down his nostrils in Misty's direction before meeting my eye and assuring me that all was well.

Over the dyke only, perhaps an old-style 50 yards away, I could see the friendly shape of the Loch Tummel Inn. It offered refreshments to the thirsty traveller and the bar window winked at me with the wicked assertion that I would never be missed for an extra five minutes.

In my haste, I almost bumped into a lady in the doorway. She looked at me with eyes like mountain tarns, deep, dark pools of Highland water. When she spoke, her lips were wood orchids awaiting the kiss of a butterfly.

"What a handsome dog", she said. "May I stroke her"?

I gave the lady full marks for getting Misty's sex right, but shook my head slowly and said:

"I wouldn't really advise it. She has an uncertain temperament and has already tried to make a meal of the postman this morning. But," I added, trying to put a bright side to things, "if you have husband trouble Misty will soon sort that out".

She gave a quick glance over her shoulder and lowered her voice to a conspiratorial whisper. "I've just got this one"!

Then, coolly and calmly, as a distinguished-looking gentleman joined us, she added, "Meet my husband, Jack Warner".

We shook hands as he remarked, "You wear the kilt for real. Let's all have a drink".

While he engaged mine host in an animated conversation about cars, I found myself, once again, looking into those lovely, lochan-like eyes.

"We're drinking Bloody Marys", she said. "Is that all right"?

I nodded. I'd never tasted one before but felt that, right now, anything would be all right. The drink tasted like tomato juice that had been laced with high explosive. I choked over it.

"Probably just a touch too much Tabasco", the lady commiserated.

When I had recovered, she continued, "Tell me, what do you do"?

"That", I answered, "is a question my daughters used to dread. I've done so many things in my lifetime, but since I started writing they just put me down as `author'".

Her laughter was the music of a hill burn as it chuckles its way over the pebbles.

"I don't suppose", I said, somewhat hesitantly but with the feeling that I was now entitled to put the question, "that you have to do much more than just look beautiful".

"Thank you", she replied. "But I have to work, too. I'm an actress".

"Really. What does it feel like to step outside of yourself and be somebody else"?

"I love it", she said. "It's my life. Do you ever go to the movies"?

"Not since I took Irralee to see `Old Smokey' on our honeymoon".

"Irralee? What a lovely name"! she exclaimed.

"It's the name of a river - and she loves horses".

"Oh, yes, I love horses, too".

"Well", I said, "this bar we're standing in was, not so long ago, stables for the stagecoach horses".

"Stagecoach - in the Highlands"? She gasped.

At this moment we were joined by her husband. "It's time to beat it, dear", he said. "There's a coach coming in and it could be full of trippers".

I hastened to assure him that it was just our midday service bus. "We call it Wells Fargo. Uncle George drives and Cousin Charlie takes the fares and rides shotgun".

There was that musical laughter again. The actress dipped into her handbag and produced a card and tiny gold pen and wrote something.

"Here", she said, "is something to remember me by".

I thanked her, popped the card into my sporran and, with Misty padding by my side, set off for home.

Walking down the road I wondered who she was. Of course, the answer was in my sporran. It read, With my very best wishes. Elizabeth Taylor.

Well, I thought, you never really know who you might meet and I groaned at the recollection of what I had said at our meeting"...if you have husband trouble".

I crept into the house and sat down at the table, hoping to look as if I had been waiting for ages. Irralee had seen or heard my approach and was rescuing the meal from incineration in the oven.

She popped a plate in front of me. "Time for you, seems to stand still at the Tummel Inn".

I stabbed a piece of pie with my fork and waved it in the air.

"As a matter of fact, I had quite a long chat with Elizabeth Taylor".

Irralee raised her eyes and gazed across at me with a resigned, almost sorrowful look on her face.

"Of all the fantastic excuses you come home with, this is the best one yet!"

My Very Good Friend Drumbuie

He started life as a small, vulnerable calf born into a Scottish blizzard. Before long, our loyalty and friendship for each other were as big and strong as my golden-haired Highlander himself...

The storm crept in silently, like a wild cat stalking its prey, before suddenly revealing itself in a snarling, savage attack of swirling snowflakes. But, storm or no storm, it was calving time and the Highland cattle had to be checked.

I tramped through the carpet of white to where I knew they would be sheltering. The Thumb was a clearing in the woods where, Highland folklore has it, a giant, on the road to the isles, stumbled and fell, leaving his thumb print among the birch trees. It was a secluded spot where not even the most vicious storm could penetrate, but was forced to fly howling over the treetops.

Fighting my way through the white clouds of snow, I finally saw the cattle, steam rising from their nostrils, as they stood in a circle in the centre of The Thumb. I counted them quickly to find there was one missing. I peered through the swirling flakes and I saw her standing apart from the rest under a fir tree, its boughs weighed down, almost to breaking point, by the burden of snow.

It was Nighean Dhubh, the Black Maiden, a young heifer with a Gaelic pedigree as long as the dark, silken hair that rippled down her sides. She was near to calving and, like most young mothers, not at all sure of herself.

In her days of growing up she had seen how the other cows, when their time came, quietly disappeared to some secluded spot. But where was she to go in this storm with the snow piled up high all around her?

She also felt the birth pangs that gripped her body and knew there was no time now to go anywhere. Already, just under her beautiful, black tail. there was a pair of legs with a little pink nose in between them.

The heifer made an agitated half circle, gave a restless toss of her head and raised her long, dark eyelashes to reveal two deeply-disturbed eyes. They looked straight at me and I realised immediately that she was asking for help. Slipping up behind her, I gripped the tiny legs firmly as she took a step forward to leave the calf in my arms. The Maiden had given birth to a son!

All this had not gone unnoticed by the other members of the herd and I could almost smell the excitement running through their hairy bodies as they gathered round to see the new arrival. This was a communal calf, belonging to them all. But Fraoch, the leader of the herd, thought otherwise. She was not carrying a calf and stepped forward boldly to take the new-born one for her own, licking it dry with the life-giving massage of her rough, warm tongue.

The Maiden was horrified and, giving vent to her feeling with a long, drawn-out bellow, advanced to claim her son. Fraoch lowered her head over the little one, ready for battle. She had a formidable pair of horns but this did not deter the Maiden who, growling her outrage, charged.

They met with a crunching crash of horns and heads and, in the battle of heavy bodies, the little one was kicked, first one way and then the other. I moved in and grabbed hold of the calf from underneath the flailing hoofs and horns and towed it behind me through the nearest snowdrift.

My wife, Irralee, appeared on the other side. When I hadn't returned at teatime, worry had sent her out to look for me. Taking two legs each, we ploughed our way, as quickly as possible, back towards the croft. Gasping for breath and with legs that could barely stagger another step, we saw the steading gate in front of us.

At this point, the calf decided to make itself heard for the first time and, with its head laid over my shoulder, almost burst my eardrums with a long, longing calling-for-Mum bawl.

The contestants heard and abandoned their battle to charge uphill after us. We almost flew the last few yards and slammed the gate in their faces. It was an old-fashioned iron gate and withstood the charge of frustrated Fraoch. The clash of her horns meeting the metal was a fearsome sound not even the howling wind could deaden.

We placed the calf on a bed of straw in the barn and, when Fraoch had given up and gone back to the herd, I opened the gate for the Maiden, who was waiting patiently. Never having had any roof over her head other than the sky, she hesitated in the doorway. But, when the calf called again, she forgot her fears and stepped inside to comfort her son, skilfully nudging his nose to her udder.

Next day, I decided it was too dangerous to allow the Maiden and her son to rejoin the herd with Fraoch pacing back and forwards, still firmly convinced that this calf was hers. So, for the time being, I kept them within the confines of the croft buildings.

The calf and I got to know and trust each other. He wasn't dark like his mother but a rich red with a colourful splash of golden hair cascading over his shoulders. I named him Drumbuie (golden back).

It was a tense moment as I opened the gate to allow him and his mother to rejoin the herd. The Maiden was apprehensive and fearful of another confrontation with Fraoch, who had made her intention clear. She wasn't kept waiting. With horned head held high, Fraoch came to meet her, circling around with her long, blond hair flowing rhythmically on her flanks. She stopped suddenly in front of the calf and, with dilated nostrils, sniffed the little one.

She then blew disgruntedly down her nose. The calf had been suckled and smelled of the black one. She wanted no more to do with it and, condescendingly, led the Maiden and her son into the herd.

When the time came for the calves to be caught and experience the restrictions of a halter it became clear that Drumbuie's temperament was not the same as the others born that season. He didn't plunge and rear on his hind legs like they did before bowing to the inevitable. He just sniffed my bare arm and the rope in the friendliest fashion and never gave a quiver as the halter settled around his head. He then trotted happily by my side like a dog on a lead.

Drumbuie grew fast into a large and impressive member of the herd and made no secret of his love for my company. He would come forward to meet and greet me whenever I approached. He always got his reward - a tickle between his huge, hairy shoulder blades - which made him growl with pleasure.

With the sunshine of summer came the season of the warble fly. They weren't ordinary flies, but big yellow-and-black-striped monsters with large, ugly heads carrying deadly lances.

I could always tell when they were on the wing. The cattle abandoned all idea of grazing or having a quiet lie down to chew the cud. They stood around nervously, listening to the high-pitched hum preceding the aerial attack that sent them running wildly in all directions with their tails in the air.

The warble flies would follow them, waiting only for the moment that the cattle tired and could run no more. This allowed them to settle and inject the seeds of their horrible maggots into their victims' hairy hides.

Drumbuie was their downfall. While the rest panicked and ran, he stood perfectly still while I spoke to him, gently stroking his golden mane then, with a swift blow from my open hand, I killed each fly that settled on him. He didn't move until the last one around him was accounted for!

I tickled Drumbuie rewardingly between the shoulder blades and he expressed his appreciation by moving rhythmically under his skin and licking my bare arm with his warm, wet, rasping tongue. We looked across at the others, now grazing peacefully, and felt very pleased with ourselves.

Life became peaceful once more for everyone and everything - until our neighbour's black Aberdeen-Angus bull literally bulldozed his way through our stout, stone dyke.

I thought I would resolve things by picking up a stout stick and waving it in the face of the intruder, but the bull didn't take the slightest notice. Without a word of warning, he charged, butting me in the chest like a battering ram and sending me, spreadeagled and helpless, to the ground.

I choked over the hot steam from the bull's nostrils as he lowered his huge body to indulge in his speciality of kneeling on and crushing his victim. I could feel my ribs giving under the pressure of his big, bony knees and a red mist was floating in front of my eyes when I felt the ground shudder underneath me. It was Drumbuie, lifting the black bull from my body with his huge horns and throwing him to the ground on his back, with a resounding thump.

The black bull rose to his feet uncertainly and ran off, squealing with terror, Drumbuie followed him to the dyke and, with another scything sweep of his head, gave him a helping horn over.

I crawled painfully towards Drumbuie, clawed my way up his side and clutched a handful of his golden mane. I then gave him the call that he had learned as a calf to come to the barn gate where his reward was a turnip, carrot or cabbage, provided he "asked for it".

Drumbuie guided my stumbling steps to the gate and bawled, loud and long. Irralee heard him and, horrified at what she saw, gave Drumbuie his carrot and organised a trip to hospital for me.

By the time my ribs had mended, the year was drawing to a close. The trees were donning their beautiful autumn dresses, and the time had come to send our best stock to the Pedigree Highland Cattle Sales at Oban. How, I wondered, could I possibly say goodbye to Drumbuie.

But our car, a necessity in the Highlands, was in dire need of replacement and the cattle, especially Drumbuie, would provide the wherewithal for another more reliable one.

The dawn's early light had changed from a cold grey to a warm pink blush when the transport arrived to take the cattle to Oban. The big cattle float backed towards the gate of the loading pen and let its ramp down, like a gigantic jaw dropping open.

The majority of the Highlanders had never been inside. They were born free, among the heather and bracken, with a bed under the stars. This is the moment when all the skills and persuasive assurance is needed to calm the apprehensive tremors that are running through the cattle, needing only the spark of a wrong movement to create chaos.

Drumbuie, however, made it all look so easy. I whispered a few coaxing words into his ear and softly patted his broad backside up the ramp as he led the others into the float. The wooden gate clicked shut with the snap of strong teeth. "What a grand lot of beasts", the driver said, relieved at the comparative ease of the whole operation. "The big one will top the market for sure".

Drumbuie had managed to turn around inside, squeezing past the others, and was looking at me through the bars of the gate. Since I had first known him as a new-born calf in the freezing cold, Drumbuie had never asked me for anything. But he was asking now, shaking his hairy forelock allowing me to look into his eyes. They glinted and glistened like the deep pools of the hill burns when they are about to brim over.

I knew in that moment that the car would just have to limp along for another year.

"Hold it!" I yelled. Forcing every word past the lump in my throat, I croaked, "Let the big one out".

Drumbuie bounded down the ramp towards me like a big, hairy dog just released from his kennel. He discarded his cloak of confinement in one earth-trembling shake and, pressing his big, moist nose against my face, he ran his rough, warm tongue up the side of my cheek, which said all he wanted to say. I could barely see the float disappear round the bend in the road, but my very good friend, Drumbuie, and I watched it go together.

All Alone On Her Wedding Day

Ginny's was a wedding that was different, and I was an honoured guest. In fact, I was the only guest...

As a young gamekeeper on a Galloway estate, bordering a long, sandy stretch of the Solway, the thing I loved most was to lay down my gun and gamebag, take off my clothes and plunge into the waters of a secluded bay. The salty sea made swimming so easy, every wave and ripple lifting me buoyantly to the next.

One morning, I had stayed in longer than usual. Wading out of the water, I was like a sleepwalker stepping out of an ecstatic dream, but reality was racing towards me in the shape of Ginny, the goat girl. She flung her arms around my neck and sobbed.

"I found your clothes lying on the beach and thought you were drowned".

I didn't say a word. I was cold, whilst Ginny's body and arms felt so warm. Then she became all practical and took off her pinafore.

"That will cover you until you reach your clothes", she said and, on the way back to where I had left them she delivered a serious lecture about the dangers of swimming in the bay.

All this left me speechless with surprise as I hadn't, before, even been on speaking terms with Ginny. I knew she looked after Her Ladyship's pedigree goats and lived at the Home Farm with her father, a widower. He cared for the prize-winning Galloway cattle. I had also heard Ginny was "walking out" with one of the gardeners.

She banished any further thoughts by going on again about the terrible tides and undercurrents that ran outwith the bay, not forgetting sharks and, she added darkly, octopuses.

I was about to ask, jokingly, if she was trying to frighten the life out of me but thought better of it, realising that Ginny was full of kindly concern and caring thoughts for everyone and everything. So, instead, I enquired why she had come looking for me.

"Well", she said, matter-of-factly, "I have a nanny goat wanting to go to the billy. My father usually attends to these things but Dad had an argument with a bull - and lost! He's in hospital with three broken ribs. So Her Ladyship suggested that I got hold of you because, she said, you had a wonderful way with birds and animals".

"Mind you", Ginny added with what seemed to be like a warning, "the billy takes some understanding".

The way I felt about Ginny at that moment, I would have fought an army of billy goats to gain her favours. Arm in arm, we made for the Home Farm, where I cautiously opened the top part of the billy's door.

The big goat was backed up against the far end of his pen with his head lowered to present a most fearsome pair of horns. Without even a warning snort, he charged, hitting the timber between us with a splintering crash. Then he reversed as if winding himself up for another attack.

"Distract his attention", Ginny hissed in my ear, "and I'll slip in the nanny".

I was determined not to show the slightest sign of cowardice in front of this girl, so I slid back the bolt of the bottom door and faced the billy in his den.

He surveyed me for a second, then charged again. I side-stepped and grabbed his horns in a cross-arm hold, such as I had seen the cowboys use to throw steers in the Western films. But it didn't work with the billy. He had a neck of solid steel.

As we wrestled furiously, Ginny led in the romantic-minded nanny. The billy goat got the wind of her right away and threw me through the open doorway. Ginny dived after me, slammed the door shut, slid the bolt home and said coolly, "There now, we'll just leave them to their love-making. Thanks so much for your help".

I rose to my feet a trifle unsteadily. Ginny started picking pieces of straw from my shoulders. Her nose twitched.

"I'm afraid you smell". She giggled. "That's the worst of being too close to a billy goat. Here, let me help you take off your jacket. I'll give it an airing while we have some tea".

As I slipped out of my jacket sleeve, Ginny was very close. Her jet-black hair brushed my cheek lightly with the soft touch of silk and, as she turned towards me, her mouth was only inches away.

I kissed her impulsively for three hectic heartbeats then drew back, shocked at myself.

"I never really meant to do that. I've never kissed a girl before", I stammered.

Ginny looked pensive and I prayed she was only pretending to be serious. She was, and teased me with a thoughtful, "Well, you didn't do so badly for a beginner"! Adding, "It's time for tea. Let's go and put the kettle on".

Her easy-going manner was infectious and I quickly forgot my momentary embarrassment. We tucked into freshly-baked scones, warm from the griddle and laced with butter that made them, literally, melt in the mouth.

"How is it you look like you do without putting on powder and paint like the maids in the Big House"? I asked her.

"Oh, maybe it's the goat's milk". Ginny chuckled. "Here, I'll put some in your tea and see what it does for you"!

It had taken me no time at all to get very fond of Ginny so, taking a deep breath, I almost shouted, "Will you come with me to Newton Stewart on Saturday? There's a Western film showing at the cinema".

She didn't reply, so I tried persuasion.

"We could have supper at the cafe afterwards".

Ginny reached out and clasped her hands over mine.

"You've just no idea just how much I would love to, but I can't. I'm getting married on Saturday morning".

"Married!" I gasped. "I didn't know".

Her voice faltered and fell to a whisper.

"I'm expecting".

"Expecting who?"

Ginny relaxed her hold on my hands as she sobbed.

"Don't you understand anything about girls? I'm going to have a baby, to Bill, the gardener".

I rose and put my arms around her shaking shoulders.

"Oh, Ginny," I blurted. "I'm just an awkward fool".

"No you're not". She gulped. "You're just a nice, innocent boy". She gazed up at me through her tears and, in a voice that held a plea for help, she asked, "Will you come to my reception on Saturday? It's at midday, here. Bill and I are to be married at the manse in the morning. The butler and the lady's maid will be witnesses".

Ginny drew the back of her hand across her eyes and looked up at me, pleading, "Please, please, say you will come".

I was a bit heartbroken myself but with well-feigned cheerfulness assured her that nothing, not even a brand-new Western film, would keep me away.

Saturday found me at the Home Farm, wearing my dress kilt. On the stroke of 12, I gave a cheery rat-tat-tat on the iron knocker and Ginny opened the door with a squeal of delight.

"How lovely to see you", she exclaimed, kissing me warmly and adding, "You're allowed that one. It's from the bride".

She looked radiant and was dressed in a smart, blue costume, a rose pinned on her bosom.

Inside, the table was candle-lit and groaned with good things. In the centre, with pride of place, sat the wedding cake, a little Cupid perched on the top.

I looked around at the empty chairs and asked, "Where is everyone else?"

"The reception has been cancelled", Ginny's lip trembled as she told me, "Her Ladyship sent a message yesterday saying she trusted' there wouldn't be a reception as this was no occasion for rejoicing or celebration.

"Bill has had to go back to work. He was told the grapes on the vines were in urgent need of thinning. I just couldn't bear the thought of being alone this afternoon. Bill agreed with me not to send you a cancellation notice and said you would be company for me".

That was as far as Ginny got. A tear trickled down her cheek, followed by a deluge of others.

I wasn't even allowed to wear my mother's wedding dress". She wailed as the sobs came thick and fast.

"I think it's all most unfair", I growled indignantly and, in softer tones, "Why don't you wear it now? I'm sure your mother would like that".

Ginny dabbed her eyes with a handkerchief.

"Do you think it would be all right?" she asked hopefully.

"Of course", I assured her, boldly. "It's your dress now, isn't it?"

Ginny didn't say another word, but bolted upstairs. I picked up a meat pie. It looked and smelled delicious, but I didn't feel hungry.

Spotting a bottle of wine nudging the wedding cake, I undid the wires on the neck and the cork flew out with a bang. The wine bubbled out of the bottle and I filled two glasses that sparkled all the way up to the brim.

By this time, Ginny appeared at the top of the stairs and came down with slow, measured steps. In her mother's wedding dress, she looked a perfect picture-book bride.

Wordlessly, I handed her a glass and raised my own.

"A toast to the bride", I announced. "Lots of happiness".

It was all I could think to say and we clinked our glasses and both took a sip.

"Do you find", I asked, "that the bubbles go up your nose?"

It was the first time I had seen Ginny smile that day. She pointed to a box camera sitting on the sideboard.

"That was to have taken the photographs". She sighed.

"Well why not"? I cried, excitedly. "Don't move. I'll take your picture".

"The dress is a little tight around my tummy", Ginny confided. "It won't show, will it?"

"Not a bit," I assured her. "You look gorgeous. Just stay still and give me a big smile. Come on, you can do better than that", I coaxed. "That's better, hold it, again, and again. There", I exulted triumphantly, "I've taken three, just to make sure".

Ginny thanked me.

"I will always treasure those wedding pictures, 'specially as they are the only ones I'll have. And now," she announced practically, "I feel hungry. Do you fancy a pie? They are really good. I had a taste when I made them last night".

"Gosh. You are a good cook!" I mumbled through my first mouthful.

When I could eat no more, I pushed back my chair and poured another two glasses of wine, remarking at the same time that this was the most fantastic wedding feast I had ever attended. Ginny's face lit up at my show of appreciation.

I spotted a gramophone, searched through a pile of records lying beside it and placed one on the turntable.

Magically, the room was filled with music.

Bowing low before Ginny, I asked her, formally, for the pleasure of this dance. She flowed into my arms, and, finding she was slightly taller than me, kicked off her high-heeled shoes before we glided round and round. The strains of a wonderful waltz wove their spell over and around us until the needle hiccuped apologetically and the music faded.

I dutifully escorted Ginny back to her seat saying, "Did you hear about the couple who were waltzing when the lady suddenly said, 'Can you reverse?'

"Sorry, he said. `Have I made you dizzy?' "Not at all, she answered. `You are unscrewing my wooden leg'".

It was so good to hear Ginny's laughter healing the hurt I felt she had unfeelingly been caused. She looked up at the clock on the wall.

"Heavens!" she exclaimed. "It's nearly five o'clock. How the time has flown. Bill will be home soon".

"Well there's one blessing", I joked. "You won't have to make a meal".

"No", Ginny agreed, "I think there's enough to keep us going for at least a week. I'd better take a chance to change into my `everyday' clothes".

I sensed the time had come to make a discreet departure as Ginny started to climb the stairs.

"I'll have to go now", I said, as she reached to top. "Thank you for such a lovely time. I have really enjoyed myself".

Ginny raced back down the stairs, her brown eyes shaded with soft flecks of sincerity.

"Thank you", she said, "for making everything right when it was going all wrong. There will always be a special place in my heart for you".

I just couldn't find anything to say so, with what I hoped was a cheerful wave, I turned to go.

Turning again, I tried to say something, finally forcing every word past the lump in my throat and, with all the wisdom of my 17 years, croaked, "Keep wearing your wedding dress, Ginny. Bill has only to see you now to know he is the luckiest fellow in the land".

Tarra's Choice

The whistle sounded, sweet and persuasive. Would the collie's affection keep her with us - or would she leave in obedience to her former owner's command?

Herding Highland cattle on foot requires a sixth sense: the ability to see the thoughts mirrored in the cows' eyes, to read every rippling muscle movement, especially the twitch caused by an excited shout or the menace of a raised stick.

Any such sudden movement usually results in horned heads being tossed this way and that and thundering hooves shaking the earth as the nervous animals make a hasty escape.

After such a desperate day, Irralee and I decided that we needed a dog who understood the moods and wayward ways of Highland cattle. We consulted our neighbour, Calum Og, the shepherd. He advised us to look for a collie whose days of leaping over the rocky, heather-clad hills after fleet-footed blackfaced sheep had slowed him down a bit - a dog ready and clever enough to relish the job of caring for wayward Highland cattle.

"Go now to the other side of the loch", Calum said. "Seumas, the shepherd there, could have the beastie you are looking for. He's a mean man with dogs and asks for everything that they've got - and more, too.

"The collies don't last long on the hill with Seumas. But be careful, now". Calum Og's final piece of advice was a request married to a command, "Seumas can be a terrible man at any time and mean with humans, too, especially when he's been wrestling with the drink and it has got the better of him, as it usually does".

We called at Seumas' house and were greeted by dogs barking

excitedly from all directions. He eventually answered our knock and did indeed look as if he had been wrestling the night before, and lost!

His head was sunk into a massive hairy chest and he surveyed us with a slight lift of his hooded eyelids.

"Well"? he asked gruffly.

"We were looking for a dog". I stammered, "that was getting too old to chase the sheep".

"My dogs never grow old".

Seumas ground the words out through twisted, tobacco-stained teeth. "Who sent you".

"Calum Og", I ventured, feeling I was betraying a confidence.

"Oho!" Seumas bellowed, suddenly coming to life. "That Calum Og was always too big in the mouth. I suppose he told you that I was sore on my dogs"?

"Indeed not", Irralee interrupted. "He said your dogs were among the best in the valley and he suggested that you might have one looking for an easier way of life".

Whilst Seumas stroked his beard, I reflected that Irralee's soft answer did indeed turn away his wrath. Seumas seemed to be thinking along the same lines and said, almost grudgingly, "You had better come in".

Bare walls surrounded a table with a whisky bottle on it. Seumas produced three glasses and filled them.

"Well now", he said, "you will join me in `my morning'"

This was his way of offering hospitality, so we thanked, sipped and awaited his further word. From somewhere underneath us came a strange noise like something, or someone, trying to speak.

Under the table lay a black-and-white collie. Seumas topped up his glass and, in answer to our unspoken question, said, "That's Tarra, the Gaelic for `white front'. She went off with the wrong dog, so I drowned the pups and took her on the hill for a big sheep gathering. She worked well enough all day, but the milk must have been too heavy on her and she's lost the use of her legs.

"One of my best dogs and now she's foundered". He gazed

reflectively. "I'll be putting her down this afternoon".

Seumas drained his glass and set it down with the sharp crack of a rifle shot. Irralee dropped on one knee beside the collie and gazed deeply into a pair of honest, brown eyes that held a desperate appeal for help. It was a plea that she simply couldn't ignore.

Irralee rose and, looking Seumas straight in the eye, said, "May I take Tarra home and try to do something for her"?

Seumas sucked a few stray drops of whisky from his beard, and thought for a moment, staring into Irralee's eyes.

"Right you are, then". He grunted. "But don't come to me for a hand in the burying of her".

Irralee loves all animals and had gained some experience at a veterinary practice in Edinburgh. So Tarra was given a deep, warm bed of golden straw in the byre beside Finoola, the milk cow. With her big, warm, generous body Finoola provided the central heating, and she loved the company!

The days lengthened into a week and, whilst Tarra was now bright of eye and the straw bed danced to the thump of her tail, her legs remained useless. One night I found Irralee sobbing silently at the fireside.

"What on earth is wrong"? I asked.

"Everything is wrong". She gulped. "That horrible man is right. Tarra isn't going to walk again. Ever"!

Sensing that this was not the moment for sympathy, I enquired, "Why are you giving up now? The dog is looking really well. She has bright eyes and a cold, wet nose. Her coat has a shining, silky gloss and she has an appetite that makes insatiable look an inadequate word".

Irralee jumped to her feet. She had wrestled night and day with this problem and had suddenly found the answer.

"That's it! Tarra doesn't get another mouthful, from this moment, unless she comes for it"!

The days that followed were too tortuous to describe. No matter how pathetically Tarra whined, the tasty titbits remained 12 inches from her nose and she was finally left with no option but to drag her useless limbs towards them.

I couldn't bear to watch any more, but dedication is a way of life to Irralee. She suffered with Tarra the agony of every stumbling step as the dog struggled towards her favourite chocolate biscuits, always placed a little farther from her reach.

One morning about two weeks or so later, I met Irralee coming from the byre. She was carrying a bucket of Finoola's creamy milk. There were stars in her eyes and, by her side, trotted Tarra!

Our days of chasing cattle were finished when Tarra took over. With her help, we could move them quickly to new pastures whenever it was needed. In no time at all, she got to know all the "breakaway" places between fields and, with split-second timing, she would be there with "no road this way" spelled out with her lolling tongue. Tarra loved the fun in life, too.

One day, when our little ones were receiving their summer swimming lessons, one of them, full of confidence of conquering the waves, made a sudden dash into the deep water and disappeared!

Tarra was there first and, when she surfaced, the youngster grabbed the long, bushy tail that had been so cleverly presented to her. Tarra then towed her to the safety of the shallows.

From that night on, Tarra slept in the house as a member of the family.

Calum Og called one morning with something on his mind. He didn't disclose it, however, until he had discussed the weather and the state of the crops. After allowing a suitable pause, he came to the point.

"I have some sheep that I just can't get to the market", he confessed. "There's an old ewe - a wild hussy - that leads the flock away up to the top of the hill.

"She defies my dogs and knocks the daylights out of them if they challenge her. I was wondering", he said slowly, his tongue savouring the sweet taste of persuasiveness, "if you would care to try Tarra on them tomorrow".

Before we could make any reply, Calum Og continued with his chin on his chest, "I wouldn't have come asking, but it's my job that's at stake. If I don't get those sheep into the sale ring"...

A friendly neighbour, even if they live more than a mile away, is someone to be treasured in the Highlands. Tarra and I were on Calum's doorstep just as the dawn was bringing a smile to the craggy hill overlooking his home.

The sheep raced off as soon as they saw us, leaping over the rocks like mountain goats with a desire to be airborne. But Tarra, moving like a streak of lightening, overtook and challenged the leader.

The big ewe skidded to a halt and stood her ground with angry, stamping feet. Tarra crept closer, with her belly hugging the rough rock, and every forward movement a study in slow motion.

The steam from the ewe's nostrils hung for a moment in the frosty morning air. She lowered her horned head and suddenly charged. Tarra slipped her body aside neatly and nipped the ewe on the cheek as she passed by! Enraged, the "Queen Of The Blackies" turned and charged again.

Tarra sidestepped at the last second again and, this time, nipped the ewe's well-padded behind. That was the end of the contest. The big ewe turned tail and led the flock down the hill into the waiting livestock lorry and the closing of the ramp completed the capture.

Only then did Tarra relax. She rolled on her back and, with delicate strokes of her forepaws, removed the wool from her mouth.

Calum Og's sheep made the top price at the auction mart and he celebrated his good fortune in the local inn. As the drink gradually loosened his tongue, he assured the shepherds around him that Tarra was, indeed, the best sheepdog that the Highlands had ever seen.

Seumas was seated in a corner, listening. His sheep hadn't done so well at the market. He rose in an ugly mood, pushed his way through the shepherds, and confronted Calum face to face.

"Tarra is mine"! Seumas spat the words out. "And you would do well to remember that"!

Calum, a big man, rose to his full height and poked Seumas in the chest with a finger like a fence post.

94

"The dog, Tarra, belongs to Croft Douglas", he said slowly. Seumas slunk back. "We'll see about that".

He was on our doorstep next morning, before the sun was up. With no niceties about the weather and in tones that brooked no denial, he said: "I want my dog back".

Irralee set her fists into her lower ribs defiantly.

"Certainly not", she said. "You couldn't look after her when she was yours".

Seumas took a backward step, shaken by Irralee's forthrightness. But he quickly recovered to play his trump card and, through clenched teeth, he hissed persuasively, "if I was to go across the burn to the March dyke and Tarra came to my call, that would surely show she was mine. That would be fair, would it not"?

There is no fairer person than Irralee. Tarra, she knew, had been trained since a puppy to answer Seumas' whistle. For a moment, she hung her head to hide the biting of her lip. Then she threw her head back, looked Seumas straight in the eye, and said, "Yes, that would be fair".

Seumas's bloodshot eyes shone with the light of a gambler sure of winning, and he set off, gleefully leaping the burn.

"I'll whistle three times", he shouted over his shoulder.

Irralee gave Tarra only two words, "Stay here", and the collie obediently flopped at her feet.

Seumas was at the dyke. His first whistle was short and sharp. Tarra's ears flew to the top of her head. The second was long, sweet and persuasive. The collie sat bolt upright. The third whistle came in a loud, piercing "Come-to-me" command.

Irralee, in her short skirt and ankle socks, looked like a little girl lost. Tarra had started forward and now, with forepaw uplifted, the dog paused to look up, desperately seeking some word from the one she had learned to trust.

But Irralee kept gazing at the sky, blinking furiously, and one teardrop escaped to pause briefly before tirickling down her cheek.

That was the moment that Tarra turned her back on her tormentor. She sat down again beside Irralee, licked her bare knee and decided for herself to whom she belonged!

Memories Are Made Of This

This week, Gideon learns that there's a first time for everything when a cry for help from Irralee conjures up wonderful memories of boyhood days and a timeless craft...

My grandfather's blacksmith's business was a large and successful one and the glow of his forge fire usually showed four horses being shod at a time by him and his specially selected trio of farriers.

There was always a long line of animals, with their attendants, standing outside, patiently waiting their turn.

My grandfather Gideon Scott wasn't a tall man, but was almost as broad as he was long and seemingly made of pure muscle.

To see him handling those huge Clydesdale work horses was like watching a David firmly but gently dealing with a host of hairy Goliaths.

I'm sure that the secret of his success with horses lay in his trick of breathing a soft, reassuring "something" into their nostrils before calling them by name.

When I ventured to ask my grandfather how he could possibly remember so many different names, he put his strong, protective arm around my small shoulders and said, "It's no secret, son. You just ask the handler his horse's name, then memorise it for a moment."

Every horse," he assured me, "knows its name and if you speak it softly, frankly and in a friendly fashion, the horse will forget fear and accept you as someone to trust.

It's as simple as that."

"Mind you," he added with a grin, "horses are just like people

- some can be more awkward than others!"

Witnessing the fitting of a red-hot shoe on to the foot of many a horse branded a bit of my mind with the searing hiss of the metal's kiss and the pungent smell from the billowing plumes of yellow smoke that set my eyes smarting with a sting that stays with me still.

Some speckled hens, with scarlet combs and powder-puff bottoms, bobbed in and out of the horses' hooves.

They didn't seem to mind the smoke or sense the possible danger of being trampled underneath those huge feet.

"It's the undigested corn they're after," confided the youngest farrier, and added with a chuckle, "it doesn't cost a ha'penny to feed your grandfather's hens!"

I thought about this as I collected the bonny brown eggs from the nests of hay in the horses' mangers.

Next morning, at breakfast time, I watched Aunt Jen cooking slices of ham in a huge iron frying-pan that hung from a hook over the fire.

She then heaped the ham to one side and, deftly cracking egg after egg, plopped them into the hot fat, powdering them generously with salt and pepper.

Then I was guided to a place reserved for "small fry" at the breakfast table and seated upon a large wooden chest in the window alcove, beside my little cousin, Gretta.

She was Aunt Jen's only child and her mother had taken a great pride in telling me that Gretta only weighed two pounds, two ounces at birth.

She was born prematurely during the war, such was her mother's shock at the news that her husband was "missing in action."

In fact, Aunt Jen assured me her baby would never have survived if the doctor hadn't persuaded Grandma, who was feeling poorly at the time, that a week or two in bed would do her a world of good, and also that the tiny baby be popped into the bed beside her for company.

Now Gretta and I sat, side by side, with our heads bowed, quiet as mice, whilst Grandfather said grace.

I surveyed the two, thick, mouth-watering slices of ham.

Then there was the egg. It looked good, well basted with an unbroken yolk, but the very sight of it brought back the smell of smiddy smoke saturated with singeing hair and hoof, and the distinctive aromatic whiff of undigested corn!

I had the wild thought of surreptitiously slipping the egg into my right-hand pocket.

But it was a new kilt jacket that Mother had bought me specially for this visit and besides, I knew little cousin Gretta's dark, beady eyes were monitoring my every movement and she would be sure to tell her mother.

So I closed my eyes and ate the egg.

Actually, it held quite a tangy, appetising taste which made me quickly devour it and the succulent slices of home-cured ham, leaving Aunt Jen with a sparkle of delight in her eyes.

These memories all came flooding back today when Irralee told me that her Arab pony, Kahli, had shoes that were clinking ominously and could be in danger of coming off.

A farrier is hard to find in this part of the Highlands, but no hurdle is ever too high for Irralee to surmount.

So she turned to me with a brightness in her eyes, which I have learned to view with suspicion, and said, "Your grandfather was a blacksmith, wasn't he? Maybe you could do something about Kahli's shoes!"

And when Irralee says "maybe," she doesn't mean maybe, but something more like "right now."

So in no time at all I found myself standing in the stable beside one of Irralee's most treasured possessions, her sleek, silvery grey Arab horse.

I tried to roll back the years and remember how my grandfather would have approached the situation.

So, first of all, I breathed a brief message into Kahli's velvety nose and called him by name then, reaching down, took a firm grip of the silvery tuft of hair behind his hoof.

To my complete surprise, he helped me to lift up his foot and I popped it, so professionally, between my legs.

But then I wondered what on earth to do next!

I had only been a boy of six when I watched my grandfather remove a horse's shoe, but I remembered that he first struck off the hooked nail points, or clenches, on the face of the horse's hoof.

Irralee was hovering in front of me, like a nurse in an operating theatre, with a selection of instruments.

There was no sharp chisel, so instead I selected something I'm sure would not have been available in Grandfather's day, a special little hacksaw.

In no time at all, it snicked through the surface "anchor" points of the horseshoe nails. The rest was easy.

With a pair of pliers I pulled the heavy-headed nails down through the shoes until they fell off.

Then I remembered just how to finish off a horse's foot with a sharp trimming knife and the fine finishing strokes with a smithy rasp.

My grandfather always called me "son" in a way I answered to as one of his own, and it was in this moment of successful shoe-removing that I seemed to feel that strong arm around me, with its firm but gentle grip on my shoulder and a soft, reassuring whisper that said, "Well done, son."

Friends For Life

You can never really replace a lost loved-one, but Gideon recalls how a pint-sized pup with a heart of gold proved a worthy successor...

Ever since my much-loved collie, Tarra (Gaelic for "white front") went to the Happy Hunting Ground, hopefully to relive the life she loved most of all, forever rounding up flocks of sheep and Highland cattle, I made the decision not to have another dog of my own, as they become too much of a part of the place.

But, in her wisdom, the lady of the house firmly believes that if something goes and leaves even a small gap in someone's life, it just has to be filled!

It seems only the day before yesterday that Irralee came home, bubbling with excitement, with the smallest, most peculiarly marked, pedigreed cocker spaniel I had ever seen, clasped to her bosom.

"This," she said proudly placing the morsel of puppy in the palm of my hand, "is a present from Shona and me."

When I tenderly put this tiny spaniel on the floor, it spun around in action-packed circles with its tiny tail "tick-tocking" twenty to the dozen.

For all the world, it looked like some kind of small clockwork toy.

Then, when seemingly wound down, it sat and looked up at me with one bold, bright eye, whilst the other glittered from the centre of a jet-black patch that perpetually shrouded it in secrecy.

She was such a merry little soul, she just had to be called Ceilidh, Gaelic for the good oldfashioned fun and joy you can have with music, song and laughter that is good for the body and soul.

So little Ceilidh was christened in a cloud of spray from the waterfall that tumbles down into our wishing well, with the fervent wish that this attractively spotted little spaniel would have a long and happy life.

A day or two later we went on our first walk together to collect some firewood, but as it was more than half a mile away to the dead hazel tree I had in mind, I carried Ceilidh most of the way.

When we got there she played happily with the chips of wood that flew here, there and everywhere as I wielded the axe.

However, when I had almost finished, a momentary glance told me that Ceilidh had mysteriously disappeared!

I couldn't believe it and immediately started to run in ever-increasing circles, but there wasn't a sign of the little spotted puppy.

With my heart bobbing about in my mouth, I raced uphill to the road where I could see a considerable distance each way. But there was nothing except a red squirrel crossing like a fiery streak of flame.

Then I dashed all the way down to the lochside, but only saw roe deer, rabbits and a cock pheasant that crowed loudly before flying up through the birch tree branches with a clatter of wings.

I just had to make for the house, get more help and confess, with head hung low, to having lost my puppy on our very first outing!

I could have cried, but with joy, as I entered the house and found Irralee sitting with Ceilidh curled up in her lap, fast asleep.

The little puppy seemingly got fed up waiting for me and toddled the full half mile home, to prove conclusively that she was not only a highly intelligent little spaniel, but as independent as her blue roan spots.

Ceilidh also couldn't resist her inborn instinct to tirelessly search for anything that she decided was well worth bringing home, especially when rewarded with a biscuit.

But then she got into trouble for picking up a fluffy chick when its mother wasn't looking!

Fortunately, my spotted spaniel has a mouth as soft and smooth as silk, so that when she eventually handed back the newly-hatched chicken, it stood up and cheeped loudly for Mum!

Ceilidh always looks so dejected when given a dressing-down and hid her face under the multi-coloured waves of curls that flowed down her long ears.

But not for long.

Our clever dog quickly realised that chickens were "out of bounds," so bounced back in the next day with a teeny, weeny rabbit, gently depositing it in front of the fire to keep it cosy and warm!

Then she sat back looking so pleased with herself and wearing such a superior smile that plainly said, "This is not a Croft Douglas chicken and I know where there are plenty more!"

By this time, the baby bunny seemed convinced that Ceilidh was some kind of fairy godmother and, sitting up, smacked two tiny forepaws together and started to wash its face.

Ceilidh has never had any babies of her own, seeming to prefer caring for other puppies that came to Croft Douglas.

She's immensely enjoyed teaching them right from wrong and, irrespective of their breed, how to pick up and retrieve the proper things with tender perfection.

Because the name Ceilidh had already been "taken", her Kennel Club registration reads "Tummel Tangle", as inspired by the Road To The Isles song.

She recently won first prize in the Veteran Class and is so proud of her red rosette.

It's Ceilidh's birthday today and my little spotted spaniel is still a trim, sprightly looking fourteen-year-old.

Her idea of a real treat is to be taken to Pitlochry, sitting like a lay in the back seat of the car, then presented with something she is passionately fond of - a packet of potato crisps!

Back at the car park, a lady asked if she could please take a photograph.

By now, I'm used to receiving such a request when visiting Pitlochry, so I picked up Ceilidh and posed!

"That's just perfect," the lady said sweetly. "It's such a lovely little dog!"

Well, after all, she is much better looking than me!

As If By Magic

The snow-capped Schiehallion gives the people of Strathtummel just a taste of things to come in the harsh Highland winter, but there's much more to this mystical mountain than meets the eye...

Schiehallion, the majestic mountain that overlooks Loch Tummel, was listed back in the year 1881 as being a "Munro," the name of the man who compiled a list of mountains over three thousand feet high.

I like to think that Schiehallion's first and foremost claim to fame is being christened in Gaelic "Hill of the Fairies" because, as Highlanders will tell you, if you climb this mountain with the blaze of the morning sun on your back, the shadow that you thought was your own suddenly seems to take leave of its senses and starts to dance a tantalising Highland fling, pirouetting around in the purple heather.

Through the years, scientists have thought up various theories to explain this phenomenon, like suggesting it's "refracted light" from the facets of ice-polished rock face.

But the Highlanders, who've never set a lot of store on what scientists say, are sure the solution lies with the wonderful way the fairies work and play.

But there's yet another reason why this mountain is a really famous Munro. It proudly bears a bronze plaque on its breast to proclaim that its dimensions were used to measure the surface of the Earth.

Which surely stamps Schiehallion as the most magical mountain in the world!

This morning has seen the first serious snowfall on Schiehallion, but it has only draped around its broad, sloping shoulders, which usually means that winter is waiting a while before bringing in something spectacular in the way of stinging snow blizzards, sheets of ice and winds like screaming banshees.

But in the meantime, a weak, wintry sun is bound to surface from the black clouds and assure you, with a shiver, that it's all been a bluff!

The hill at the back of our house might one day be a Munro, because every time I climb it, mostly to search for some straying Highland cattle, I pause to place yet another stone on the cairn that crowns Creag Mhor.

Not being a Munro doesn't seem to bother the Big Rock, to translate its Gaelic name.

It just sits there, either bathing its rugged face in the bleak sunshine, or getting it slapped by freezing snow while its nooks and crannies give so much shelter to the wildlife.

For a variety of reasons, the fertile slopes of Creag Mhor are not grazed during the summer by sheep or cattle.

But now that all the ground birds have brought up their families and the wild flowers have ceased to bloom, the dense growth of hill grass and long, sweet heather shoots are in need of pruning.

These provide tasty, body-building bites for the Highland cattle before they are taken down to the sheltered lochside fields for the worst of the winter.

Pausing to savour the view of Strathtummel spread out so breathtakingly below, I notice that there are two extra animals in the herd.

It's a red deer hind with her calf, and she has apparently come down from the forestry plantation because there is always danger there in the shape of sharp-shooters.

So the red deer, with the handicap of a late little one, has wisely sought shelter and safety with the herd of Highland cattle to share a plentiful supply of food both for her calf, which has now learned to graze, and herself, to make the much-needed milk that the young one still needs.

The hind slipped away at my appearance and shyly hid behind a silver birch tree, but not her sturdy little son.

He stood his ground and stared me straight in the eye, showing no fear.

I could see the two tiny bumps on the top of his head showing that, one day, he would be a big royal stag.

Ceilidh, my little spotted spaniel, was entranced by this handsome young red deer, and moved forward to meet him. Then they had an intimate, nose-to-nose talk with each other.

It's at moments like this I wish I could have a camera in my hands, but I know that, to the wild ones, a camera lens pointed their way is likely to appear as menacing as the barrel of a gun.

So I leave this moment for my mind to record, consoling myself with the thought that I have pictures I can develop and bring back to life with the point of my pen.

Meanwhile, Ceilidh and the young buck have grown even friendlier. With forelegs spread wide apart, they seem to invite one another to have a really boisterous game then, spinning round like colourful Catherine wheels, they end up in a sprawling heap together!

It's all good fun that the young ones, wild and domestic, share for a few magical moments.

Today, I received yet another long letter from Nigel in New Zealand.

I try to explain that I can't correspond regularly, but he tells me cheerfully that it's all right because he reads my reply every week in his mum's "My Weekly"!

Nigel pens pages and pages about all the happenings in his part of the world, and it's never dull reading.

One day he is hoping to make his fortune panning for gold nuggets, or working in the forests with diagrams showing how to climb trees effortlessly using steel-tipped "jigger boards."

Nigel is also fond of food and would like a recipe for "real leek and tattie soup." In exchange he offers a suggestion of his mum's on how to make mutton chops more mouth-watering!

Just slice off surplus fat, place on silver foil in a baking dish, pour over the juice of four oranges plus two tablespoonfuls of Worcester sauce, then lightly season before folding the foil to seal the juices in.

Allow to marinate for four hours, then bake slowly in a moderate oven for an hour or so.

"This makes the chops so sweet and juicy," Nigel assures me.

Apparently there has been some rotten weather in Nigel's part of New Zealand but, by now, he should be bathing in sunshine, whilst we face our winter.

However, Nigel sums it all up so nicely by saying,

> *Whether the weather be cold,*
> *Or whether the weather be hot,*
> *We will weather the weather,*
> *Whatever the weather,*
> *Whether we like it, or not.*

Making Hay

They're making hay while the sun shines up at Croft Douglas this week, with the swish of the scythe and the sweet smell of summer in the air.

When the summer morning is mirrored in minute detail on the surface of the loch and there are fragile fragments of mist drifting daintily here and there, like the cast-away wrappings from a gift, it's a beautiful sunny hay day. And, as the flinting dewdrops are drying, fanned by the breath of a light morning breeze, we carefully sharpen our scythes, with old Finlay's words ringing in my ears.

"Laddie, you'll never scythe until you can sharpen." He always calls me laddie, and it keeps me years younger than I am.

So the stone slides caressingly up one side of the blade and down the other, as we carefully sharpen the scythe to cut the hay the old-fashioned way.

There's a host of wild-life in our little hay field. They are the fortunate few who won't be terrorised by the rough, raucous chatter of a reaper.

The soft whisper of the scythe says slowly, and regretfully, that it's time for all furred and feathered folk to find shelter somewhere else.

There's a pair of partridges who have nested here. They're moving about just in front of the blade, so I pause to give them a little time to think things out and make their next move.

The cock bird steps out first. You can always tell him by the bold chestnut coloured horseshoe stamped on his breast and, with a quick right and left look, decides that the time has come to conduct his family to pastures new.

He gives a soft, reassuring "churr" to his mate and out comes the hen, surrounded by what looks like a host of multicolored bumble bees. She wears a more modest dress, cleverly designed to camouflage and deceive predators, but she still manages to look pretty with her feathers preened to perfection.

Partridges are among the best parents in the bird world. The cock bird takes his turn to look after the large family whilst his mate has a well-earned "wander" and forgets, for a while, the demands of domesticity and the calling and caring for children.

She just happens to discover a patch of tares, the wild pea with the velvet violet and white flower. They are now at their sweetest best and, like any lady lured to a box of chocolates, she isn't sure when to stop, but she does, to indulge in a luxurious dust bath in a sandy molehill pre-heated by the midday sun.

She sifts every grain of sandy soil through her feathers and sighs at the thought that she mustn't overdo things and keep her model husband waiting too long.

For today is serious stuff, the family has to move and the parents, between them, carefully shepherd their children to the nearby "steep" field. It has not been cut this year and there is plenty of grass and clover to give their babies cover from high-flying hawks.

Young rabbits race out at regular intervals. They are almost half grown and out on their own. Mother is expecting another batch of babies!

But the young rabbits don't mind, they're experiencing the exciting feeling of independence and treat this sudden moving of house as a huge piece of fun.

There's a dainty roe deer fawn suddenly awakened from a short sleep, unsure where it is and what is happening. But Mother is watching and waiting by the woodside.

With a series of short, sharp barks she guides the frightened fawn to the safety of her side.

I pause again for a moment to survey something just in front of the scythe's next sweep. It's a pair of leverets lying side by side, like little furry slippers, their velvet ears lined with pink that seemed to be buttoned to the small, silky, brown backs.

The only movement is fractional, just a nervous twitch of a tiny nose.

So the scythe carefully cuts a sheltering circle around them. The mother hare won't be far away and, on her return, will find her babies till safely tucked in the cosy cradle she so carefully made for them.

Visitors from the South are more than a little amazed by the long light of day we have here in the North, and providing the weather is kind, haymaking can be carried on throughout the momentary shadow that is sent at this time of year to represent night and dulls the glint on the hay forks for just a second before the dawn takes over and shakes the shoulder of the sun who, literally, hasn't had a wink of sleep and reluctantly rises again to supply yet another sizzling hot hay day.

Although the grasses are still green, like the preparation of a good meal, they must not be exposed to intense heat for the risk of burning. So, as soon as it's dry, we toss the green grass on to tripods of strong birch branches and build a series of conical coles which will preserve the goodness of the grasses, while the birch branches invite any passing breezes to go in and cool the heart of the cole and prevent any internal heating of the hay's juices.

Sometimes, when our hay crop is not a heavy one, we have to buy baled hay, made the commercial way. You only have to poke your nose into the baled hay shed, then into the barn of the carefully collected grasses, to know the difference.

Our hay was a sweet, seductive smell, so fresh and wholesome. No wonder the Highland cattle race to be first at breakfast when the snow is deep on the ground.

How they savour every mouthful and taste again last summer's sunshine. And, when it's finished, they turn to the "leaves" of baled hay as something to, fastidiously, nose about and toss over their shoulders before partaking as a filler-upper.

Today, I have to take time off from the haymaking and catch the train at Pitlochry, to see someone in Stirling. I had a chat with the train guard, a young fellow full of fun, with long hair that curled up in a glistening black roll at the back of his neck.

As I got out at Stirling he leaned out of the window to exchange a last few words when a young lady dashed forward and panted, "Is this the train for Glasgow?"

I stepped back to allow the guard to deal with the question, which he did coolly, using his customer placating voice.

"It's the next train in. You'll have to wait only a few minutes."

While the girl thanked the guard, I had time to admire the gleaming, blonde hair that hung all the way down her back. Then I found myself listening to their further conversation.

"I'm going back to Stravanger, but first I have to get a real souvenir - a Scotsman's hat."

The guard immediately clapped a hand on his. "This one," he said, "belongs to Scotrail."

"But what," asked the girl, "if the wind blew it away?"

"In that case," the guard replied cheerfully, "I would be supplied with a replacement."

The maiden's feet quickened to keep pace with the moving train.

"I have never," she confided, "been kissed by a Scotsman," and held up her face with the invitation etched on her red lips.

"Only to happy to oblige, miss," declared the delighted guard and lowered his head. For one fleeting moment their lips met then the train snaked around a bend and disappeared.

The girl stood waving a last goodbye and in her hand was the guard's hat!

She turned towards me, beaming brightly, but I tried to be stern with her, saying, "Your ancestors came to Scotland, pillaging and plundering."

She was entranced and exclaimed, "How exciting!" Just to emphasise my point, I added darkly, "They even carried off Highland woman." Her eyes opened wide.

"You mean," she gasped, "I could have Highland blood. How wonderful, But do not worry about the train man."

She laid her warm hand on mine.

"He will remember the kiss long after he has forgotten his hat."

I had the feeling the young lady was right. She was a very lovely-looking Viking.

Magic Moments

Christmas has always been a particularly special time for children but, even now, this once-a-year day has lost none of its magic for Gideon and the other inhabitants of Croft Douglas.

I was brought up to believe that the magic of Christmas belonged chiefly to the children and indeed, as a small boy it was the most terrifically exciting time of the year. Christmas Eve was the beginning of a night that had no end.

If I ever slept it must have been fitfully and I was probably a sore trial to Santa Claus before sheer exhaustion overtook me and allowed him to fill the kilt stocking hanging hopefully over the brass rail at the end of my bed.

I was awake again long before the dawn and could never understand how I had missed the magic moments of Santa's visit. I knew he must have come but, just to make sure, I crawled down the bed in the darkness and ran my fingers over and around the bulging contours of my stocking.

Then, shaking with excitement, I reversed noiselessly back underneath the bedclothes and squirmed impatiently as I knew it was forbidden to take out the contents until the clock chimed seven! It was then that I learned the sweet joy of anticipation.

Hamish's house lies almost in the lap of the loch, at the water's edge. His farm has a lot of flat land, a rare commodity in Tummelside.

Now that he has retired, Hamish can indulge himself in what was always nearest to his heart - to have a herd of horses all of his own. How he loves to spend endless hours watching them running free, and appreciate the poetry of their every movement.

They race each other, stretching their long, supple legs to the utmost in a fast and furious gallop through the shallow waters that rise in a fine film of spray to the insistent beat of the horses's hooves, surrounding them with clouds containing a million sun-tinted bubbles.

To Hamish, all are notes in a symphony of sweet music that he could listen to as long as the day lasts.

But today the rhythm of the racing was disturbed because the fastest animal was the only mare and she had taken time off to have a foal in a sheltered spot by the lochside.

To Hamish's utter dismay, the wayward mother rejected her little one and left it in a pathetic heap whilst she went to rejoin the others and continue racing.

Hamish knew that Irralee shared his love for horses and immediately enlisted her help. Together they caught up with the mare and shut mother and son together in a small stable so that they could get better acquainted.

But the mare still wanted nothing to do with her new-born baby and snapped angrily at any attempt it made to search her flank and try to suck.

This left the foal staggering about weakly, on long wobbly legs, and Hamish in the depths of despair.

Irralee, however, has never been one to accept defeat without a fight, and she immediately set about searching the valley for something in the way of a foster mother.

The chance of finding someone with a mare who had lost her foal was just a forlorn hope, and cow's milk, which flowed plentifully everywhere, was not really suitable for newly-born foals.

But Irralee wasn't to be denied the daunting task of saving this young life.

She is a great believer in the properties of goat's milk and heard that Betty, in her croft high on the hill, had a nanny who had just given birth to a single, very small kid. Betty said this must be because it was winter as Fanny usually had twins at the very least.

Irralee lost no time in persuading Betty that her goat could possibly save a little foal's life and transported the nanny and her tiny baby to Hamish's stable and told him exactly what he had to do.

Hamish was clever with his hands and quickly constructed a table with stout legs and sloping ramp that Fanny could trot up and stand on the tabletop with her full-to-overflowing milk bar nicely placed near the foal's nose.

The hungry little one soon "latched on."

Fanny's milk still contained the "beastings" or colostrum, so vital to put the lining on the foal's tummy, and soon the stable resounded to slurps that spoke for themselves.

That evening I called back at Hamish's to take Irralee home. A shaft of light shone from the stable.

Irralee was standing in the doorway with her eyes shining, whilst Hamish sat in the straw watching over the foal and little kid curled up together beside the manger, making a never-to-be-forgotten Christmas scene.

It's Herka the Samoyed puppy's first Christmas, and sure to be a white one as long as she's around!

When it comes to wondering if Santa Claus will visit on Christmas Eve, all the Croft Douglas family are believers, starting with Ceilidh, the spotted spaniel.

She knows from past experience that her stocking will contain a big bone and delicious extras like chocolate drops, and she sees to it that Herka will become a believer, too, by finding a sock from somewhere and placing it in front of the pup's bewildered black nose.

My daughter, Shona, spends Christmas Eve moving about Croft Douglas in a mysterious, surreptitious manner throughout the evening.

Christmas morning dawns with magic in the air and makes me a believer, too, as I crawl down to the bottom of the bed and find my kilt stocking hanging there. Irralee is busy doing the same thing at the other side.

We both sit back and excitedly open the goodies contained in our stockings, starting with the highly-coloured cracker at the top.

It's then the years roll back, and we are boy and girl again.

113

It's In The Stars

Gideon scorns the star-gazing that Irralee sets great store by, but is forced to eat his words after a couple of close encounters...

Irralee will gracefully admit to having a certain amount of superstition, like being careful about walking under ladders and viewing Friday the thirteenth with more than just a hint of suspicion.

Neither will she open an umbrella indoors or bring honeysuckle, hawthorn or peacock's feathers into the house.

On the other hand, a black cat crossing her path paves it with good luck.

Then there's the weird and wonderful ceremony of welcoming the new moon.

I appreciate that this is a purely private and confidential affair, not to be witnessed by anyone not taking part.

But still, I can't resist peeping through the gap in the curtains, whilst trying not to feel bad because it's my silver Queen Victoria crown that Irralee has clutched in her hand.

This is because she believes that the new moon will have nothing to do with modern money and will only smile kindly upon those with solid silver shining in the palm of their hand.

The climax of this elaborate ceremony comes when Irralee pirouettes slowly and gracefully around, three times for luck, with a bow to the brand new crescent of light at the completion of each turn.

I stopped smiling tolerantly at all this display of superstition the day I found myself being careful not to step on the adjoining lines of the stone slabs on Pitlochry pavements.

Irralee also makes no bones about being convinced that our future is influenced by the position of planets and stars, and she always looks forward to the predictions of her favourite astrologer.

This morning Irralee pointed out his special page to me and, in particular, the paragraph titled Aquarius.

Then she accounced, "It says here that it will be a quiet week until Thursday, when something really exciting is going to happen to you!"

When Thursday came around I smiled to myself as I set out for Pitlochry to get some supplies and thought how harmless all this business of trying to read the stars really was.

I had just completed purchasing pony, poultry and dog food - the animals and birds always have the highest priority on the shopping lists - although I did manage to include something tasty for our midday snack, too.

As I crossed the main road I saw a car coming towards me at high speed and I raced the final few feet to the other side.

Suddenly the car swerved to avoid another one coming the other way, and struck a glancing blow to my side, sending me and the shopping sprawling in front of Pitlochry Post Office.

I jumped up just in time to shake my fist at the driver who was being chased by another car which also swept past at a furious rate.

Both vehicles sped out of town in a haze of blue smoke, and I could only assume that my assailant was being pursued by an unmarked police car.

When I returned to Croft Douglas, Irralee remarked how fortunate I was to have been wearing a kilt.

Its thick, hand-woven pleats had taken the brunt of the blow, leaving me with nothing more than an aching right side and a big black and blue bruise on my hip bone.

Irralee dressed it with a massage balm containing birch leaves which, she convinced me, works wonders with bad bruises and has curative properties all of its own, while telling me gently to pay more attention, in future, to what the stars had to foretell.

Although she did admit that what had happened wasn't exciting, but downright dangerous!

The morning was one that heralded heat for the day, the mist first covering the lochside in a deep, dense, woolly white curtain that, having descended, seemed to delight in taking its time before slowly and tentatively lifting to reveal a glimpse of sunshine and blue skies above.

The morning mist was still barely off the gound when I set out to check on the cattle.

They seemed restless, only grazing spasmodically and pausing, now and again, to look up nervously.

I looked up, too, and could hardly believe my eyes!

Drifting down out of the mist was a little golden-brown figure with wriggling body movements that danced about, trying to control silky cords attached to something that looked like a gigantic golden butterfly with a double set of gossamer wings, suspended from a pristine white canopy that kept coming closer and closer!

At that moment I felt sure that the little brown figure was someone who had "baled out" of a flying saucer.

This was even more than really exciting!

It's not so long ago that Robin, a forester who lived at Allean, near Loch Tummel's Queen's View, had a sighting of a flying saucer, even pointing out the scorched circle it had left when landing and taking off.

I had never doubted him and now felt sure I was about to meet one of the saucer's crew for myself.

The Highland cattle, which had clearly had enough of this strange creature from the sky, took off with a thunder of hooves and their tails in the air.

No wonder! They were the first to hear the "talking" of a radio transmitter that now dangled down on the end of a long line just in front of my face.

I was sure that I was expected to say something and thought I'd better shout to overcome the thumping of my heart.

I didn't even recognise my own voice when I said, seriously and slowly, into the silvery antennae that dangled and danced before me, "My name is Gideon and you are about to land on Croft Douglas," adding as an afterthought, "this is friendly territory."

The transmitter then landed at my feet, followed by a limp little brown body which seemed so tired and lay down in a soft bed of clover with just a twitch or two.

Seconds later, the big gilded butterfly alighted gracefully, as if just wishing to give its wings a rest. And, last of all, the snow-white parachute settled like some gigantic mushroom.

I went first to the little brown figure, but realised by its limp and lifeless attitude that it was just a helpless heap of rubber.

What worried me most was that stencilled in bold, black letters across the "body" were the words "HIGHLY INFLAMMABLE"!

Then I had a closer look at this soft, pliable, almost human shape and decided it was a thick rubber balloon which had finally burst, and all its agitated movements when descending had come from the escaping hydrogen.

When I picked the transmitter up, it was still warm and had a card attached to it which read, plainly and simply, "This is the property of the Berkshire Meteorological Office."

I could only hope now that the transmitter didn't tape human voices or that its battery was dead. Otherwise I would have given the Met. people quite a laugh!

What signs do the heavens hold tonight, I wonder?

Away to the west there's a shape of a gigantic arrow in the sky.

It's a skein of wild geese flying in "vee" formation, their shadows silhouetted against the red and gold of the setting sun.

Small Wonder

While the upwardly mobile Gideon is moving in high places, courageous granddaughter Little Irralee is growing up fast and doing him proud...

When the wild greylag geese, who spent the winter with us, finally gathered together and flew away in vee formation like a flighted arrow speeding across the sky, back to their home in Spitzbergen, they left behind a young couple who had made the daring decision not to return, but marry and have family here in the Scottish Highlands.

The pair of young geese were surveying a sheltered, sandy bay by the lochside as a suitable place to set up house when I decided to cease observations, believing that even birds should be left in perfect peace when having a honeymoon.

Today, Little Irralee, our delightful granddaughter, has suddenly grown up, at the tender age of seven, by giving herself her first insulin injection.

This takes, I am sure, the kind of courage that is never marked by a medal. The reward, in this case, comes from doing something for yourself that will make the difference between living and dying.

Little Irralee had a serious accident when she was 17 months old which resulted in her becoming diabetic and requiring an injection twice daily.

Her mother also had to keep a close watch on her diet, with mealtime amounts very carefully measured and scrutinised for quantity and quality.

I remember, too, when Little Irralee was just a toddler, she wore a blue ribbon around her neck, threaded through the ring of a disc which declared in bold, block letters:

I AM DIABETIC. PLEASE DO NOT GIVE ME SWEETS.

The trouble was, she was such an attractive little girl with something especial about her smile, which was surrounded by tiny golden curls that tumbled and jostled about, joking with each other at every shake of her head.

It was no wonder that some folk were tempted to offer her chocolates, but they only had to heed her upturned face and blue eyes, beaming with serenity as she said the words her mother had "dinned" into her, "If I eat sweets I will die."

This would have caused some battle-hardened RAF types I knew to break down in tears. There were also big fellows who ignored the Orderly's advice and looked at the needle when being given multiple jags for anti-this and that, then fell down in a faint!

Little Irralee's mum has made sure that she doesn't have to feel handicapped, by encouraging her to take a big part in the things she loves doing, dancing and running.

So today finds her with many well-merited Highland dancing medals.

At the School Sports Gala Day and Highland games, Little Irralee competes in the races, running like the wind with her golden hair streaming behind.

She beats many others bigger than herself and usually ends up breasting the winning tape with the best.

Up to now my daughter, Gillean, has done the necessary "needle work", but if she was out when the clock hands pointed to the vital time, or couldn't manage for some reason or another, brother Kevin, although not so very old himself, administered the dose with a delicate, sensitive proficiency that might suggest an eventual career in the medical profession (although he seems to think he might be a mechanic!)

Ceilidh, my spotted spaniel, and I spent a little leisure time roaming around Croft Douglas this afternoon. One of our stops was at the tall tree that has a missel thrush's nest at the top.

My spaniel seems to sense that I am tempted to climb and sits down to watch with interest.

I have the feeling she believes I'm a bit crazy but, I'm sure, in the nicest possible way!

I think that climbing trees is a pleasurable short cut to heaven. As I make a further foothold at the base of the next branch, I embrace the tree trunk with my left arm, and with my right hand, reach for the sky!

The missel thrushes are perched next to each other on a neighbouring tree regarding me with a diffidence that suggests they have something to hide, and indeed they have.

There are four eggs in the nest!

They look so pristine - pale blue with reddish brown spots that have soft, sand-coloured shadows.

Much as I would like to, I daren't touch the eggs. That would break the bond of trust between myself and the thrushes who already know me from the time I spent watching them build their nest.

I am glad of our "peace pact" as I retreat, step by step, to put my feet back on the ground, because these birds are mighty atoms when it comes to defending their home and can attack with such ferocity that even a curious, climbing wild cat is forced to flee ignominiously.

The pair of young greylag geese are drinking from the placid waters of the bay, which gives me some seconds to look for their nest. But it's Ceilidh with her soft, super-sensitive nose who finds it first.

It's a neat circle of dried grass under the shelter of a sandy bank, bordered with bunches of bell heather, and Ceilidh looks up at me with a "Guess what's here?" expression in her warm brown eyes.

Carefully, I part the camouflage coverlet to expose eight pearly-white eggs.

It's such a thrill to find the first wild birds' eggs in another new year.

There's something about them that holds so many promises, just like the plant growing beside the goose's nest, with tiny green, fresh fingers on the hand that reaches from its heart, opening out to reveal a posy of golden primrose buds and the promise of life beginning all over again.

The Northern Lights

There's chaos at Croft Douglas, but it all proves worth-
while at lighting-up time...

At Croft Douglas, even today's increased quarterly bill does
nothing to diminish the ecstasy of flooding our home with electric
light on a dark night, at the flick of a switch.

When we first moved into our Highland home, just after World
War 11, kindly neighbours presented us with two storm lanterns
filled with paraffin, a bundle of candles and a box of matches
which, they assured us, would give at least some sort of light on the
dark winter nights.

With the first money we made, by selling a litter of twelve fat
little pigs at the market, I purchased amongst other essentials an
Aladdin-type lamp, complete with mantles and paraffin.

This was surely something in the way of a big improvement,
being able to work by its soft, glowing light.

But there was one big snag - it wasn't suitable for taking outside
because, when a breeze blew down its long glass globe, it behaved
like a very active volcano.

So when our first Highland calves were sold, we bought two
Tilley lamps. They were very up-to-date, but still depended on
paraffin.

However, when vigorously pumped, the Tilleys produced a
brilliant light and, what's more, they had handles so they could be
carried from room to room.

But we still had to depend on the old-fashioned storm lanterns
for outside use.

Their light scarcely wavered in the highest wind as we made our way to the byre at milking time, or to bed down the ponies in the stable.

I still liked to write by the light of the Aladdin. You had to move very close to it, but the mantle glowed softly, sympathetically and soundlessly compared to the constant hissing sound of the Tilley lamp.

But it was a Tilley lamp that welcomed one of our little ones into the world by worshipfully wafting its light up and down and then suddenly going out!

The District Nurse was a martinet with a capital M and I never, ever thought to hear her call for help. But she did, loud and clear, when the lamp went out.

I immediately dashed to help, carrying our other Tilley. Its light revealed Irralee picking up and cradling her newly born babe.

But that's all I was privileged to see, because the nurse bundled me out of the bedroom, hissing in my ear much louder than the Tilley lamp, "You shouldn't, and wouldn't ever have been in here before they were presentable if it hadn't been for that blinking lamp!"

And the way she said "blinking" left me in no doubt as to exactly what she thought of our lighting system.

Then, power and light-wise, we progressed still farther by having gas installed. This provided us with light and a cooker so that at last we could get rid of our Primus stove and the clinging, persistent smell of paraffin.

But, of course, there was the need to have a new container of gas delivered regularly to replace the empty one.

Then came the day I approached the Hydro Electric Board whose poles, carrying electricity to the South, cross our land at the foot of Creag Mhor.

I was told that, although this power from the Tummel waters was passing near by us, it would be a complicated and costly business to supply Croft Douglas.

It would involve a fixed sum of money to be paid over a period of seven years, after which we would only pay for the electricity we used.

Although we thought this was a bit unfair, considering Croft Douglas was next to and assisting the source of the power, we banished all thought of a windmill or a do-it-yourself wheel in our waterfall, and decided to sign up for the seven-year payment plan.

From then on it was all action.

Early one Monday morning, three large trucks drew up at our door. The first one was full of men who spilled out like an army going into battle.

They all wore the same uniform, topped off with protective tin hats.

The next vehicle was loaded with long, heavy poles and the third contained a huge green metallic box with long, curling, insulated antennae, making it look, for all the world, like some flying machine from another planet!

It was carried on the back of a caterpillar tractor that trundled its way through a prepared gap in the roadside fence, then waddled slowly but surely straight up the hill towards the nearest main-line post.

A little later, two men with red flags took up their position on the road to stop any traffic when they got the signal.

I thought this was taking safety precautions a bit far as the gang was now at work at least a quarter of a mile up the hill.

But suddenly a banshee-like sound filled the air as a siren wailed its warning and, seconds later, simultaneous explosions sent the wood pigeons skyrocketing.

Huge chunks of rock were hurled high into the air, to hang there momentarily before raining down like giant hailstones. Some of the smaller boulders bounded down on to the road, but the flagmen casually cleared them away before waving the traffic on its way.

This went on for a week before the last holes were blasted through the solid rock to connect us with the main power line.

At dusk, when the men had all gone home, I climbed the hill to see what they had done, but was diverted by the sight of a big bird feeding on a dead fox, lying in a patch of snow.

It was a young golden eagle, one of last year's chicks, now having to fend for itself. Carrion is a last resort but will keep it alive.

The eagle stretched out its huge wings to rise, but I immediately turned round and retreated to show I meant it no harm.

It was good to see a young, fully-fledged golden eagle ready to grace the skies of the Scottish Highlands.

Word quickly scorched the heather tips, especially from the power station at Tummel Bridge, that we were ready to be "switched on".

Folks came from miles around to witness this great event and, at a signal, Irralee and I tentatively flicked the switches that flooded Croft Douglas with light. Gunshots were fired and everyone cheered themselves hoarse.

It was such a happy occasion.

This cold winter's night there's an electric blanket on the bed. It's so toasty and warm and the bedside light goes off at the flick of a switch. Sheer bliss!

On The Up

While two lonely hearts are looking for a mate, there's a rich reward when Gideon hits the high spots of Strathtummel.

There's a magical sound in the air this morning and it's coming from a small circle of silver spruce trees bathing their feet in the shallows of Loch Tummel.

It's a sound I find so difficult to describe - sweet and noisy by turns with a rolling, rhythmic repetition, like a drumstick being repeatedly drawn, with great deliberation, across an old corrugated iron roof.

It's the call of a cock capercaillie, the name probably derived from the Gaelic "horse of the woods."

I haven't seen one for some considerable time, so it's really something to hear this huge, proud Highland turkey.

Scotland's biggest game bird, calling for a mate.

I really hope that he is successful and that there is still a hen left who can hear him.

In Scotland, capercaillies were hunted to extinction around 1762. They were then re-introduced to this particular part of the Highlands in 1837, the birds being sent from Sweden.

The Swedes had some to spare, having looked after their capercaillies more carefully.

The new stock from Sweden seemed to like life here and re-colonised much of the Scottish Highlands.

Sadly, since then, the number of capercaillies has not only declined but, in these parts, it has been decimated to the extent that even the Scottish Environment Minister has expressed his concern and invited comments.

The regal capercaillie and the dainty roe deer don't have many friends amongst the forestry fraternity, because they both sometimes feed on the shoots of young trees, especially conifer.

Why, I wonder, shouldn't they? Being vegetarians, they are only eating something that the good earth will keep providing for time immemorial.

This is one of the most exciting times of the year with everything beginning again.

The sight of a glittering cluster of crown jewels would, for me, fade into insignificance compared to just a look at a wild bird's nest of newly-laid eggs.

This sometimes leads to a lot of climbing up to the top of a great spruce tree where the branches are thickest and their countless sharp needles keep stabbing at head and hands.

But the reward is rich - when you reach the top you see a sparrowhawk's nest with five eggs that have an untouchable look.

They are so beautifully speckled and, just like finger prints, no two are spotted in exactly the same pattern.

Scaling the rocky mountain crags is a different climb, but there is still the same urge to reach upwards to where the kestrels have their nest in a secretive rock cleft which holds the clutch of russet-red eggs.

They haven't got a new-laid matt finish but are very highly polished and almost ready to hatch.

I'm sure of this because, for some time now, the hen bird has been hugging the eggs close to her breast and turning them twice a day with a careful, caressing movement.

The climb gets much more difficult as I go even higher to have a look at the golden eagle's eyrie.

Amazingly enough, despite their formidable talons, the eagles have adopted an almost casual, couldn't-care-less attitude about an approach to their nest.

This is maybe a ruse to mislead an intruder, but it doesn't seem to help when their eggs and fledglings are taken by unscrupulous collectors.

It's now I find myself looking up at the parent birds floating high overhead, like two dark rain clouds.

I can't help wishing I had wings, too, because that's the only way I'm going to get close to their nest. Instead, I have to be content with a distant sighting of two white, downy eaglets, like lively little snowballs.

As I climb down the rocky crags - and, believe me, it's often a lot harder coming down than going up - it's good to feel my feet, at last, cushioned by the clumps of heather that lead downhill and through the silver birches.

Here, on the highest tree, there is a mistle thrush's nest. I would like to call the cock bird a close friend of mine, because he sang through the February snowflakes in honour of my birthday.

But I know better than to stretch the bonds of friendship too far by going near the nest with its four fully-fledged chicks.

The mistle thrush knows that it's now his family is at its most vulnerable, when they are about to take their first flying lessons and, with a shaky landing, could lose their balance to flutter from the safety of the treetop and fall to the ground.

It's in this moment, fraught with danger, that the mistle thrush becomes a mighty atom, quickly driving away a cunning carrion crow, seven times his size. Or a prowling fox is also mercilessly beaten about the head until he is forced to flee.

Then the gallant little thrush shows his tender touch by tempting his "crash landed" chick with a titbit, which it gets as a reward for following him, branch by branch, back to the treetop.

The mistle thrush is surely a supreme example of courage in a fragile frame of speckled feathers or, as the old Scots saying goes, "Guid gear gangs in sma' book."

I had walked more than a mile this morning, inspecting the Forestry deer fence that marks the boundary of Croft Douglas, when Ceilidh, my little spaniel, came running towards me. From her air of excitement I knew she had found something.

So I followed her tick-tocking little tail and there, just ahead, I saw something that looked exactly like an outspread fan with beautiful colourings of brown and cream.

It was the finely-pencilled flight feathers of a hen capercaillie that fluttered helplessly at our approach.

I could tell at a glance that she had tried to creep through a hole in the fence made by a badger and a stray loop of wire had snared her by the leg.

She didn't seem to realise that Ceilidh and I had come to help her and dealt me a stinging blow with her beak on the back of my hand.

I quickly wrapped the big bird in my jacket whilst I unwound the wire from her leg. I then set off down to the lochside, with the hen caper still nestling in my jacket and Ceilidh dancing at my heels.

With a hand placed gently but firmly on each wing, I placed this beautiful bird on a silver spruce branch where she sat and watched me with her fire-flecked brown eyes.

Then I gave Ceilidh a hand signal and we both crept silently out of the capercaillie's sight.

Extinction, like the snuffing out of a solitary candle, sounds so final.

How I hope that Ceilidh's discovery and our combined efforts to bring those magnificent Highland turkeys together are successful and ensure a secure future for the Strathtummel capercaillies.

Out Of The Woods

When Drumbuie and company are left high and dry, it's
time for a moving experience...

The big stags are not roaring now since the rutting season
finished some time ago, but I can see them moving downhill with
the rest of a large herd.

These reddish gold, regal creatures wear antlers and coronets
like ivory crowns that bob about as they nod their heads with each
forward step, leaving the footprint of royalty stamped in a fresh fall
of snow.

The red deer are seeking the lower ground for shelter and
something to eat, while snowy-plumaged ptarmigan, the hardy hill
grouse, and white hares will stay in their mountaintop homes
whatever the weather.

Both are small enough to burrow under the thick, bushy blanket
of heather to escape the icy blasts of blizzarding snow. They
survive by finding food there, too.

We are on the hill this morning to collect our Highland cattle.

They normally wouldn't be up here at this time of year, but
summer grazing had to be delayed considerably thanks to the
programme of planting forests on the hills in this part of the
Highlands.

The trees have grown bigger and bigger and are therefore
claiming a much larger supply of water, chiefly through their stout,
thirsty, "tap" roots.

So when the summer sun is shining and there is lots of lush
grass and sweet young heather tips on the hill, we can't put the
cattle there because there's not a drop of drinking water!

The merry little mountain burns that used to chuckle on their way downhill have been silenced and sucked underground to satisfy the thirst of thousands upon thousands of trees, leaving only a pitiable pebble pathway, studded here and there with multi-coloured pieces of quartz, to mark the tracks that the hill burns used to take.

That's why we sometimes have to wait until the autumn showers get the hill burns flowing again, although they're still just a trickling shadow of their former selves and often barely enough to slake the thirst of some hairy Highlander.

But this year, because of early snowfalls and icy frosts, the cattle will have to come down to the lower lochside land where there will still be some good winter grazing, to hopefully last the old year out and see the new year in.

There are also native trees down there who have a kindly outlook on life, with an offering of lush woodland grass lying at their feet as a supper snack before the tired beasties bed down for the night under the shelter of the big ash trees with outstretched arms.

Directing Highland cattle down a heathery hillside, through a maze of big silver birch trees, is not a task for the faint-hearted, because these beasties re akin to the wild ones who have only the sky for a roof, clouds to claim as blankets and twinkling stars for night lights.

But having now got the herd moving towards the road, that's where the greatest hazard lies.

The crossing gates at either side have to be opened at precisely the right time, at a second's notice and a given signal.

All traffic must have ample warning to stop as soon as possible and so avoid the strident squealing of brakes or shriek of tortured tyres.

But by far the biggest menace is a nerve-jangling motor horn, set in motion by some frustrated driver who simply doesn't want to stop.

One of life's lessons is that moments like these just have to be anticipated and I have found, through experience, that the answer lies in a song, soothingly sung.

In those vital moments it works wonders with cattle, instantly calming down any agitated creatures, large and small.

Hymns are definitely in great demand as far as the Highland cattle are concerned.

I will always remember the sweet, innocent, sincere voice of a young boy who had been given strict instructions to start singing when things seemed to be going wrong.

Two verses of "Rock Of Ages" saved what could have been a disastrous situation, leaving all the older drovers without a dry eye among them.

Today, it was a soft rendering of "The Old Rugged Cross" that saw all the cattle safely across the road.

Being so pleased with the way they had been successfully conducted to the lochside fields, we completely forgot about the current fluctuations of Loch Tummel waters, until just about teatime.

Robin, who has a lochside croft about a mile away to the west, phoned us to say that some young Highland cattle had called at his house and were now heading uphill.

Fortunately Shona was here to help, so we piled into the car, raced along the road and were just in time to conduct the wanderers back to Croft Douglas.

Dorcha, a young bull with ambitions, was the ringleader but no doubt Drumbuie, who had been bawling anxiously all the time the youngsters had been gone, will deal with him in his own way.

They are all back on the hill tonight until we get things on the lochside sorted out.

As I left them I saw the bell heather flower with its cerise, lip-like petals framed in a fleck of frozen snow.

There's a saying that, "When the whin is not in bloom, kissing is out of fashion."

I believe that a kiss from the bell heather flower will never go out of fashion and will last a lifetime!

You're The Tops!

*Gideon has a vital role to play at the Grandtully Gala Day,
where a faithful friend does him proud, and he recalls the
time when he began to suspect that he was one of a kind...*

When I was born I was named after my blacksmith grandfather,
Gideon Scott. This didn't cause me any thought until my schooldays,
when I searched around for some boy with the same name, without
success.

It was the same in the halcyon days I spent gamekeeping on the
Galloway House Estate and the moors of Kirkowan. And there was
still no-one of my name in the boardroom or among my employees
when I was a company director.

When I was twenty-two, I volunteered for war service with the
RAF, and the medical man said, "Well, we haven't had anyone
called Gideon before."

I travelled south to Warrington and Wiltshire, then over to
Ireland, from Belfast to Newtonards, Notts Corner, Lisburn,
Aldergrove and then flew back to Lincoln, Lakenheath and North
Creakwells-on-Sea, still with no result regarding someone with a
similar name.

Then one day, just a year or two ago, I was attending a show and
sale of pedigree Highland cattle at Oban with six young Highland
heifers, when the head stockman strode towards me waving a show
catalogue and shouting, "You've got the same name as myself,
Gideon!"

I knew just how he felt as we shook hands.

Then the stockman turned to his assistants and said, "Give these
heifers a special wash and brush up."

In the sale ring my heifers swept around me like thoroughbred horses, holding their heads and beautifully burnished horns high. They looked so glamorous with their Titian-red curls shampooed and set.

Buyers from all over the world bid for them and it was a proud moment when they topped the sales at the show.

It's Grandtully and Strathtay Gala Day. Irralee and I always make time for this annual event, the proceeds of which ensure the upkeep of the recreation park and sports ground.

I am Master of Ceremonies, which sounds so important, but simply means that, for at least two hours, I am slave to a microphone, first to introduce the VIP who will say some well-chosen words, then to declare the Gala Day "open!"

Today the VIP is a lady who acquits herself very well with a short, stylish delivery. Then, together with her husband, she judges the fancy dress parade.

I have the dreadful feeling they don't realise the dangers involved because, in the front row of spectators, I can see the fond parents anxiously watching every moment with eagle eyes.

There are Mickey and Minnie Mouse, little green gnomes, silvery-white fairies with wands, witches on broomsticks, and a kelpie wheeling in a mermaid reclining on a soft bed of seaweed.

I think the VIP and her consort must be out of their minds in agreeing to take the risk of judging this long line of dressed-up youngsters but, at the same time, feel they have made a wise choice in selecting the cuddly teddy bear in striped pyjamas for first prize.

When I finally announced the full results, to my great relief, everyone, including the doting parents, applauded wildly.

So I went on quickly to announce the "world famous" Vale of Atholl Pipe Band, which swept into the arena with tartan plaids flowing, and marching to the magic of the pipes and drums.

Following gracefully behind was the colourful tartan team of Jean Swanston's Highland dancers.

Meanwhile, Irralee is fully occupied as manager of the dog show that has proved such a popular addition to the Gala Day.

Valerie, our second eldest daughter, is dedicated to the task of teaching children in an Edinburgh school and takes great pride in the achievements of her pupils.

Her husband, Heinz, is a scientific officer, who specialises in studying and sorting out blood samples.

Both love their work, but are delighted to do something different today, like helping Irralee with the long line of people waiting to enter their pets for the show.

Herka, Irralee's now-white Samoyed, is barred entry because Irralee if officiating, but that leaves the way clear for my little spaniel, Ceilidh.

She has never been in a show ring in her life before, but I know she is looking good, with her silky, spotted coat shining, because Irralee spent so much time grooming and trimming her last night.

I cannot leave the microphone, but Valerie has volunteered to lead my little Cocker Spaniel around the show ring because they know each other so well.

The pipers, drummers and Highland dancers have played and danced their hearts out and it's time, just before the races and tug-o-wars start, to introduce Douglas with his expertise on the accordion and the gift to set folks' feet tapping.

The stirring selection of Scottish tunes gives me a much needed breather.

That's when Valerie comes over, cuddling Ceilidh in her arms, with the exciting news that she has just won a first prize rosette!

Valerie also whispered to me, just in case it would hurt Ceilidh's feelings, that it was won in the Veteran's class, but I'm sure it didn't matter a jot to the little spotted spaniel.

Nothing could stop her tail tick-tocking twenty to the dozen, because she was so proud of winning a prize for the first time in her life.

I had no idea that so many men read "My Weekly" until I began to receive letters from them.

Lo and behold, one I received lately was written by a Gideon Scott from Lockerbie!

It seems, too, that we can both claim "Muckle Mouthed Meg" as an ancestor.

This is because a daring young man named Scott crossed the border one dark night and took some cattle that didn't belong to him, and in the chase that followed he was caught.

Sheep or cattle rustling was a capital offence in those days, but the handsome young Scot was offered his life in exchange for agreeing to marry the cattle king's daughter, whom all the eligible young men in the area had rejected because, they said, her mouth was too big!

So Meg moved over the border to marry into the Scottish family, and the marriage was blessed with love, understanding and little ones.

The lucky Scott escaped the gallows tree to live a long and happy life with a wife worth her weight in gold, which all goes to show that it's no misfortune to have a big mouth, just as long as the heart is warm and in the right place.

You've Got A Friend

Five new arrivals at Croft Douglas bring joy to the heart of a long-time resident...

How is it, that sometimes the hands of the clock go round so fast and bring the day so quickly to a close, leaving a multitude of things I meant to do, still undone?

But this day is different. It seems, somehow, to take a positive delight in almost standing still, often employing a series of delaying tactics before deigning to make the slightest move and, even then, deliberately dragging one second behind the other.

That's probably because I am a bit on "tenterhooks," wondering how my daughter Shona is coping with her first ever attendance at a Pedigree Highland Cattle Sale.

I know just how anxious she is to succeed in bringing back a suitable "buddie" for Drumbuie, and keep reminding myself that she couldn't be in better, or more understanding, company than John, our farming neighbour giving good advice in one of her ears, whilst Alistair from Glen Fincastle whispers his knowledgeable "do's and don'ts" in the other.

And, for the summing up of any situation and the making of a decision, what would the world do without the never-failing asset of Woman's Intuition!

It seems such a long time since we saw Shona off to Oban and there can be no thought now of having even a quick forty winks.

The dogs are always the first to hear a person approaching, or a car drawing up outside. How I envy their sensitive, inbuilt system of receiving sound. It's second to none, and they are always right!

Herka and Ceilidh race each other to give Shona a rousing

welcome, with a rapidly delivered sequence of exciting nose-to-ear conversations, finishing with a series of, "I'm forever your friend" face licks while I wait, ever so patiently, for an account of exactly what happened at the Highland Cattle Sale.

I wondered if I were to try a whole-hearted, no holds barred, doggy welcome would I be among the first to be encircled by warm, tender, loving arms!

But, eventually, Shona surfaced to say, "Oh, Dad. What have I done!"

Well, I didn't know yet, but could hardly wait to hear her next words, which were, "I've bought five!"

Before I'd even time to ask "Why?" Shona went on to tell me with the fast flow of a river in flood that, just before the sale, a beastie had been selected as being the best one for Drumbuie; a golden yellow, newly weaned calf, with a kindly, friendly look in its eyes.

But, when the little curly haired, yellow calf bounded into the sale ring like a live teddy bear, there were two other Titian red ones with him, and they all stood like little, lost children and cried for their mothers.

It was at this moment that John and Alistair, seated one each side of Shona, whispered simultaneously into the nearest ear, "They won't be sold singly. The bid has to be for the three."

And, after a series of nerve racking seconds, the auctioneer, with a traditional smack on the rostrum, looked in Shona's direction and said, "Sold."

There was a second or two of silence, during which time I could only tentatively say, "I thought you said five!"

To which Shona replied brightly. "I'm just coming to that," and went on to tell me how, almost immediately afterwards, two calves had come into the ring, looking more like wild-eyed roedeer that had been rounded up.

"Alistair told me they were from the Island of Coll and probably hardly knew humanity, but said they would soon settle down to grow like mushrooms on the lush Strathtummel lochside land, and

John added from the other side, "Their father's here, too. What a handsome, big, black, bull he is."

Shona, who never does anything by halves, heard Alistair's soft, persuasive Highland hiss in her ear, "The bidding is slow. They'll be a bargain. Go for them," adding as an afterthought, "if you've got any money left!"

"So", said Shona, "that's the way it was. The young Highland calves from Coll were just meant to come to Croft Douglas, too."

It only took me a moment to gather my scattered thoughts and say, "I'm sure you did well. It's high time we had a transfusion of young Highland blood here, especially from the Islands."

To my further question, "When are they coming?" Shona's eyes danced delightedly as she teasingly sang, "The teddy bears will be here tonight, and you're sure of a big surprise!" then said she would go to bed but wanted to be wakened on their arrival.

By this time the sun, too, had long since gone to bed, leaving a blood red glow in the sky, a sure sign that, weatherwise, it would be a wonderful day tomorrow.

Waiting for a long-distance cattle float to call can be something like watching lots of kettles coming slowly, and consecutively, to the boil.

But, at exactly quarter past twelve, our dogs barked and roused me from my forty winks, as I heard the hiss of a huge vehicle drawing up outside.

Irralee, who must have been the most wide awake, darted quickly outside. I was next upon the scene in time to hear the driver say to her, "This has just got to be Croft Douglas. My headlights spotted it spelled out in the iron work on the top of your gates."

A "floatman" has to be both a good driver and something special in the way of a stockman because, day and night, he has to handle all sorts of animals. Some of these may be apprehensive, or even agitated, and others so scared they could, with the wrong approach, become downright dangerous.

This floatman was no exception. He soothed human beings and animals alike with his quiet, confident, reassuring way of going about things and enquired, "Will that gate swing out on to the road?"

I demonstrated that it did, and the floatman's final words were. "That's good. They'll go straight through your gateway."

Shona came racing downstairs in her dressing-gown, just in time to hear the patter of tiny hooves coming down the float's lowered, wooden ramp. Our single outside light gave us a brief glance of the bobbing "teddy bears", sticking together like burrs, as they disappeared into the darkness, in the direction of the lochside field.

"Isn't is exciting," said Shona. "I can't wait until the morning!"

I pointed to a thin bright pencil line of light drawn across the sky, low down in the east, and said, "It won't be long."

It wasn't. I had barely fallen asleep when the full light of another day was with us.

From the bedroom window I could see Drumbuie. He always likes to stand and look at Schiehallion, The Hill Of The Fairies, first thing in the morning.

There was not the slightest sign of our new arrivals and we eventually found them lying together, bedded down amongst the bracken in the lochside woods. We coaxed the calves at a slow, steady pace back uphill in Drumbuie's direction, and the silver birch trees, trembling with excitement in the morning breeze, reached down with their leafy fingers to titivate the curls on the teddy bears' backs as they passed by.

When Drumbuie saw his five new companions, our big Highland bull just couldn't believe his good fortune and gave a joyous, welcoming, bellow.

And there wasn't a dry eye among us as the little calves gathered around him to claim him as their father.

Just Champion!

Herka the Samoyed revels in all the pampering that's needed to get her ready for her big moment, and Irralee is proud as Punch when all her hard work pays off and Herka the magnificent steals the show...

Ceilidh, my little black and white spotted spaniel, still looks ridiculously young, even in old age.

In fact, some folk say she must still be a puppy and make Ceilidh's long ears shoot up to the top of her head with pride.

Ceilidh has never had babies of her own, but that doesn't seem to cause her any concern, because she has spent the best part of her lifetime bringing up puppies that didn't belong to her in the first place.

Being a little spaniel with a big heart, baby-sitting became second nature to Ceilidh, although she still manages to find time for some of the fun things in life, like playing hide-and-seek with lively rabbits bobbing about under a blanket of bronzed bracken and collecting eggs from the henhouse and bringing them home, one by one, with a mouth as soft as silk.

Sometimes Ceilidh suffers a sense of frustration when a hen sits too long on the nest.

Then she reassuringly slips her nose under the bird's breast with a swaying, sensitive movement of her velvety muzzle, which leaves the hen crooning contentedly whilst Ceilidh is retrieving her egg!

But Herka, Irralee's Samoyed puppy, just has to be Ceilidh's greatest triumph.

This one wasn't the easiest to rear, having a seemingly

inexhaustible supply of energy, combined with a compulsive urge to hang on, playfully, to her adopted mother's long ears!

Ceilidh would reward her with a corrective "nip" to demonstrate the difference between right and wrong, which made the little white one sit down and think things over but, afterwards, she was always welcomed back to nestle into Ceilidh's warm, comforting body with the assurance that "Mother knows best."

We have a robin's nest, with four fully-feathered youngsters ready for their first flight, at the bottom of an old bramble bush just above the wishing well.

The parent birds are busily flitting to and fro with all manner of tasty offerings to pop into the ever-open mouths.

This is a labour of love for these robins, who lost their first nest, so painstakingly built in the grass bank beside the burn.

Just when their home was completed and contained four russet brown eggs, an angry April sky sent down a deluge, filling the mountain burn to overflowing and washing the nest, with its precious contents, away.

But robins are resourceful little birds and didn't spend much time crying over misfortune. Instead, they got busy and built their happy home much higher up.

The moorhen didn't have any headaches with the heavy rains, because she built her nest at the highest water line on the burn bank, then very cleverly moored this raft-like construction to strong roots on the burn's overhanging bank, so it would rise and fall in the face of flooding waters and provide a safe haven for her precious eggs.

When alarmed, a bird of the lochs and lakes will sink down in the water, leaving only the tip of its bill above, so it can breathe, and remains like this, motionless, until the danger of a predator has passed by.

These "preventative measures" remind me of the day I heard a commotion coming from the bathroom, and went in to find that Herka was below water - in the bath!

I couldn't bear to watch as Irralee and Shona went through the rigorous ritual of preparing a Samoyed for the show ring.

It was such a detailed demonstration of just how to wash something to make it turn out whiter than white.

Ceilidh, of course, had to take more than a passing interest in the bathing of her baby, cocking her head from one side to the other, as her ears went up and down like pendulums on an old-fashioned clock that just can't make up its mind what time it is.

And when the soap flakes fluttered down on her baby with the force of a blinding snowstorm, Ceilidh was so shocked that her spots seemed to be in danger of falling off!

The only "bathing" she had ever experienced was a quick shower under the waterfall below the wishing well or, what she loves most, a lazy, relaxing swim in the loch, when her long ears are such a help and float out on either side like decorative water wings.

But this bath business was different and didn't seem to Ceilidh to be a natural way to have a "dip", especially afterwards when the hair driers came into action!

My spotted spaniel and I both share the same dislike of these peace-destroying machines.

The moaning sound of a vacuum cleaner just about sends us mad, but these high-pitched, space-gun-like hair driers made us both slink away silently from the scene which, amazingly enough, Herka seemed to be enjoying to the full.

Next morning, when Ceilidh and I saw Herka again, we both had to admit that the transformation was startling.

With her pink, strawberry-tinted tongue lolling out, she looked like a large, laughing snowflake with a jet-black nose!

As she reclined in the rear compartment of our car, like a Royal princess, Irralee and Shona looked so happy as they set out for Perth and Herka's first show.

My final words to them were, "Don't worry. The judge will have to be `snow-blind' not to see she's something special!"

Time doesn't hang heavily around here because there's always so much to do. Besides, I had promised to look after the ponies.

When he's feeling full of fun, Kahli, the Arab, can be a bit of a handful, but wouldn't harm a fly.

Prince, on the other hand, positively hates men but makes me an exception, maybe because of my kilt!

So it seemed no time at all until the car was nearing the Croft again.

Irralee and Shona are so alike in some ways and both speak with a machine-gun-like delivery when excited.

To top all that, this time they were also triumphantly waving a red first-prize card and a red rosette to go with it. Then another! And another!

Herka had won all her classes, against many other breeds, but now found it had all been a bit exhausting and flopped down beside Ceilidh's warm, comforting body.

Through the years I have learnt to translate Ceilidh's confidential whisperings, delivered with her cold nose nuzzled in my ear, and now I can tell by "lip-reading" the movement of her muzzle that she is assuring Herka that it would have mattered naught to her if nothing had been won.

She would still be so proud of her beautiful, snow-white, adopted daughter.

Talk To The Animals

Gideon likes to keep up with all the latest news from around the Strath, and what better way to get it than straight from the horse's mouth!

The mistle thrush must be the boldest member of the society of song birds and the male bird the most optimistic as he sits on the topmost branch of a silver spruce tree, singing his heart out.

It matters not to him that the snow has been built up into a blinding blizzard by a bitterly cold west wind, or that the freezing snowflakes are sticking to his speckled breast.

It's because of his extraordinary behaviour that we call this brave bird the Storm Cock and, come rain, sleet, or snow, the mistle thrush continues to sing, "It's going to get better."

Then, when the west wind has blown itself out of breath and the storm clouds stop racing across the sky, clearing a space for a shaft of sunlight, the thrush changes his tune to a cheerful ditty directed to all doubters. "There now, didn't I tell you, didn't I tell you?"

The mistles seem to be the first song birds to mate and build nests in the Highlands, often before the end of February, and that takes a lot of courage.

There's a pair of these big-hearted birds building a nest this week, right at the top of a mountain ash down by the lochside.

Today, I was tempted to climb and look at their latest construction, and before I knew it I was on my way up!

With each foothold on a stout branch near the trunk and my hand reaching for the sky and finding yet another branch above, I leave the years behind until at the top, for a treasured moment, I become a boy again.

The thrushes' nest is nearly finished. It's quite a bulky structure, built of birch twigs and lined attractively with frosty green fronds of lichen and the beginnings of a blanket woven from blackface sheeps' wool.

I know the birds are watching me and that mistle thrushes will fiercely attack all intruders, great and small.

So, to show them I mean no harm, I don't touch the nest and start to make my way down the tree again.

Connie, Irralee's Irish mare from Connemara, is every bit as hardy as our Highland cattle.

The other ponies are rugged up during the cold winter days and wait for night to fall so that they can seek the warmth of their stable.

Connie, on the other hand, can't stand a lot of confinement and prefers to spend the night under the stars with the cattle for company, and reports with them in the morning for a breakfast of beet pulp, bruised barley and meadow hay.

Connie loves our after-breakfast chat and does this by placing her soft, velvety muzzle against the side of my face and, in Irish morse code fashion, puffs alternate jets of warm air from one nostril, then the other, into my ear.

It's a ticklish, never-to-be-forgotten experience and leaves me convinced that Connie, at some time, has kissed the Blarney Stone. Not only that, but nuzzled it closely!

I first crossed the sea to Ireland when I was posted there after a period of intensive RAF training.

It was raining cats and dogs when I arrived at Newtownards aerodrome and I was guided towards two mobile kitchens with a narrow alleyway between them.

As I passed with a plate held hopefully in front of me, a fried egg flipped through the air and made a perfect "belly flop" landing beside a huge hunk of bacon thrown with precision timing from the other side, whilst the rain tried other tactics and started, spitting viciously in the hot gravy surrounding my "offering", as it grew greasy and cold.

The dining-room consisted of a leaky tent with a rickety table on trestles that were on the point of collapse and, sitting there, in an expectant circle around me, were all the cats and dogs it had been raining.

Afterwards, I was presented with a pair of blankets and directed to a deserted old sock factory at the edge of the aerodrome.

The walls were decorated with a green mossy slime that dripped down to make mildewed puddles on the flagstone floor.

A young lady in uniform looked through the doorway, that had no door, and said in a soft Irish accent I could have listened to all day, "I'm a member of the medical team detailed to look after servicemen in the area."

She then took me home to "Mum" who gave me a sumptuous meal and sleeping quarters in her best bedroom.

In the morning, Mum told me that her daughter, Maureen, had received an urgent call in the early hours and had to leave for duty in Lisburn, but not before she had contacted the aerodrome and been assured that "works and bricks" had just finished building a billet for the airmen.

This morning, when Connie "spoke" to me, her Irish eyes were smiling and reminded me so much of the nice Newtownards nurse.

That's What Friends Are For

Gideon has to take some preventative measures when the kind-hearted Mary-Anne falls foul of some "hocus-pocus" and some errant otters step out of bounds...

Wild otters are shy, elusive creatures with magic and mystery surrounding their every movement.

I was still in my teens when I first made the acquaintance of sea otters on the shores of the Solway and, particularly, in the little loch that lay next to Palmallet farmhouse, which was part of the many miles on my gamekeeping "beat" in Wigtownshire.

From the top of the Cruggleton cliffs, on a clear, sunny day, I used to watch the otters lying on their back in the sea, blissfully sunbathing while being gently rocked to sleep by the rippling waves.

Only their forepaws twitched occasionally, trying to sort out some tickle on their tummies.

All this sense of relaxation and the position of the sun served to remind me it was about midday.

Palmallet was the end of my beat to the west, and what better place to call at than the farmhouse where the word "hospitality" must have originated.

The farmer's wife had a creamy complexion and rose-tinted cheeks.

Her only "make-up," she maintained, was an early morning ten minutes of vigorous face splashing with ice cold water, which created a natural beauty that, I thought, might cause cosmetic manufacturers considerable anxiety!

Mary-Anne was also a wonderful cook, who seemed able to

turn the simplest of ingredients into a mouth-watering meal.

On this particular day she wasn't wearing her usual sweet smile as she answered the door.

She waved her arms about agitatedly while explaining how, only that morning, when she was out collecting the ducks' eggs, a "water demon" had made her prize Aylesbury drake disappear before her very eyes and she hadn't seen it since!

And yet, despite her obvious distress, Mary-Anne still managed to produce a bowl of beef broth and a baked scone, hot from the girdle.

In return for this, it was the very least I could do to help her out.

At Palmallet, the loch lies only fifty yards or so from the farmhouse and is a sanctuary for the greatest and most colourful variety of wild fowl I have ever seen.

There are mallards, widgeons, pintails, shelducks and shovellers, so named because they have an inbuilt sifting system in their broad bills, which sorts out and rejects the debris whilst retaining what's good to eat.

Then there's the tiny teal ducks, which whistle so cheerfully, and the diminutive divers - golden-eye, tufted and pochard.

Mary-Anne's big flock of ducks are there, too, sticking their whiter-than-white tails in the air whilst they are guddling in the mud down below.

I knew just how much they meant to her, as the proceeds from the sale of their eggs gave Mary-Anne the opportunity to purchase her favourite magazines every week.

Living in this out of the way farmhouse, she had become an avid reader, confiding that she did this at night by going to bed early with her well-stocked supper plate and supply of magazines, nibbling and sighing over the stories.

Now I definitely had to do something. So I followed the outlet of water from the loch which gradually grew narrower, pouring through a tunnel in the big drystane dyke that was built on the clifftop, before cascading down the rocky cliff-face into the sea.

This, I was sure, pointed to the path the sea otter had scrambled up to gain easy access to the Palmallet loch.

Wading almost up to the waist in the tunnel, I found an iron gate lying in the bed of the burn.

It was matted with moss and rusted red, but still serviceable, and it fitted the tunnel entrance perfectly.

I felt sure that it had been used to preserve ducks, wild and tame, by preventing them from reaching the sea and allowing only the water to flow peacefully through.

I didn't feel I was starving the otter of food by closing the loch off as there were shoals of fish in the sea.

I then went back to the farmhouse and told Mary-Anne to be sure to shut the ducks in at night and her troubles would be over.

I knew the big otter, denied his easy access, wouldn't risk an overland crossing, at least until the darkness of night and, even then, there was the big dyke as a barrier.

Meantime, I had a wee talk with the poultryman at Galloway House and, by the greatest of luck, he had a young pedigree Aylesbury drake who was "surplus stock."

So the poultryman tenderly placed the big bird in the game bag on my back and I set off.

The miles back to Palmallet slipped away under my stride and, in no time at all, I was knocking on Mary-Anne's farmhouse door.

When she opened it I took her by the hand and, almost secretly, said, "I've got something to show you!"

When we reached the lochside, I undid the straps of my gamebag and, like a magician, produced the magnificent Aylesbury drake and placed him on the grassy bank near the water.

He was so appreciative of gaining his freedom again and, standing straight up on tip-toes, flapped his wings three times, then spoke.

Drakes have little in the way of vocal chords and can only softly say their name, "Drake, drake" twice, just in case you didn't hear the first time.

The flock of ducks heard all right, and flew in a flurry of spray to meet him!

149

Ducks do all the talking and, with excited, vociferous quacks, they were seemingly quite convinced that their lost mate had returned.

So, brushing his breast feathers with their beaks, they escorted him to his rightful place as their leader on the loch.

Mary-Anne turned towards me, her eyes glistening, and swept me up into a bear hug.

"You're just a laddie," she said, "but so kind and thoughtful."

I was very embarrassed and suffering from semi-suffocation, but she felt and smelt so warm and friendly that I decided that this was probably better than being able to breathe!

At the moment, we have a pair otters in the lochside bay at Croft Douglas. Their home, or holt, is well hidden under the roots of an old oak tree that hangs over the water.

They have two plump, mischievous kits and the family have great fun together sliding, one after the other, helter skelter down the slippery bank to splash into the loch.

Then the bounce back in a cloud of spray to do it all over again...and again!

Tonight, in the moonlight, I can hear the heart-stopping sound of the otter whistling a love song to his mate, and I am privileged to get a glimpse of them writing words to the music, together, with magical movements that scarcely raise a ripple on the surface of the water.

Eyes On The Prize

While the bitter winter winds force Gideon to come in from the cold, champion canine Herka can't afford to lose her cool...

For some time now, Irralee and Shona have been preparing Herka, the Samoyed, for one of the last shows of the year, where she will meet tough opposition in the shape of top-class dogs of her own breed.

Samoyeds are working dogs which, Irralee says, should be sturdily put together with strong bones for their speciality of sledge-pulling, brains for herding reindeer, and a dense undercoat to keep out the cold.

According to Irralee, too much heat will cause Herka to shed her woolly thermal underwear that is so essential for the showring.

We mere humans have spent many November and December nights crouching ever closer to the bright birchwood log fire.

I, for one, have been wearing an old-fashioned Scottish "semit" or vest, covered with a heavy, hand-knitted fisherman's jersey, matching scarf and woolly bonnet. I may even have to top all this off with my sheepskin overcoat!

In stark contrast, Herka reclines on the cold, stone doorstep like a snow queen on her throne, with the front door wide open.

She seems to revel in having her coat sparkling with frost and spangled with snowflakes that swirl in and settle here, there and everywhere.

Herka is also cultivating a canine singing voice, which is second to none, especially when there's a full moon.

She sits bolt upright, raising her muzzle to the sky with

rounded, jet-black lips, making mournful wolf music.

It's haunting and eerie - the kind of sound that, on hearing the first few notes, you just have to listen whether you like it or not!

This is, indeed, the true call of the wild ones, all about being born free. It's an exciting song that tickles the short hairs on the back of your neck until they stand on end.

Irralee sighs and says, "I could listen to that wonderful sound all night," while I, despite all my warm layers, find it difficult to make any comment when my teeth are chattering!

I have never been one to go to bed early, yet on these cold days I am not slow in seeking some additional warmth beneath the blankets at night.

Herka spends most of the daylight hours outside and positively revels in the frost and snow, skidding down the frozen patches of ice on her tummy, wearing the smile that Samoyeds are famed for!

Herka takes naturally to helping round up the Highland cattle, which she does so sensitively.

She seems to know full well that they dislike aggressive dogs, and adopts a well-mannered approach which the big, hairy beasties really appreciate when being guided along the proper path.

The Samoyed is also an expert in sledge work and Herka looks a perfect picture in her harness, pulling a load of logs on a light sledge over the deep snow that even our hard-working "buggy" gets a bit bogged down in.

The important dog show is only a day away. Herka knows all the preparatory signs and goes into hiding, but to no avail.

She is eventually tracked down and coaxed, with titbits, all the way to the bathroom, where Irralee and Shona lift her unceremoniously into the bath.

This is the moment when Herka seems to resign herself to the thought that, if this is what it takes to be a beauty queen, she just has to learn to enjoy all the preparations for fame.

She must accept the bathing and shampooing, although she already tolerates the banshee howling of the hair driers and the endless sessions of combing out the tiniest tugs.

It's an early start at the crack of dawn on the show day.

Irralee and Shona are acting like excited schoolgirls, and even Herka is wearing a happy look, because she does love a car ride.

So I wish them luck as I wave goodbye. Then I suddenly decide what I am going to do this crisp, clear, frosty morning.

I'm going to climb Meall Tarruin Chon, Hill of the Ptarmigan, and get a glimpse of those mysterious birds who live on the top of this mountain and turn white in the winter whenever the snow starts to fall.

I had a feeling that, had Irralee been here, she would have put her foot down at the very suggestion but, as they say, "When the cat's away, the mice will play."

So I set out in my little boat and rowed swiftly to the other side of the loch, then legged it past Frenich Farm House to a forestry track that provided a short-cut through a plantation of pine trees.

When I finally left the woodland behind I found myself in a white world where the chill mountain air stung sharply with every indrawn breath and escaped in puffs of steam.

Suddenly two winged snowballs swept over my head and landed in spurts of snow in front of me.

This was what I had climbed to see - this mountain's most beautiful birds.

Being unused to mankind, the ptarmigan fearlessly watched my approach, then finally disappeared, leaving only the outline of their flight feathers traced in the snow.

I managed to get back to Croft Douglas in time to greet Irralee and Shona on their return.

Their eyes were shining ecstatically in the gloaming as they held aloft the big silver cup Herka had won. It bore a bold inscription: "Best Coated Bitch."

Well, that really brings some heat to my heart and makes all the shivering worthwhile. But I am really looking forward to the front door being shut and a warm house for the rest of the winter!

Make Yourself At Home

*While the new arrivals at the Croft agree to differ, Gideon
recalls how he got more than he bargained for when he went
dealing in gold...*

This morning the sun bounced up from behind the mountains
like a bright yellow ball to give a golden start to what promised to
be a beautiful day.

It's then I am reminded of an Aberdeenshire farmer, to whom
a life insurance agent was trying to sell a policy.

He told him how happy his family would be that he had made
such provision for their future, when the day came that he was no
longer around.

To which the old farmer replied, "Laddie, when I go I would
like it to be a very sad day for everybody!"

But it does look like being an exceptionally lovely day for
everybody today.

Our newcomers, the cluster of calves that came to Croft
Douglas from the big sale at Oban to keep Drumbuie company, are
settling down nicely, thanks to all his fatherly feelings, caring
attention and sound advice.

He guided the little ones to where to find the tastiest herbal
titbits on the banks and braes of Loch Tummel, he showed them the
shadiest place to lie down on a lazy, hazy, summer's day when the
sun is high in the sky and he pointed out that the most sheltered spot
to spend the night was in a cosy circle around his huge body, which
generates so much heat that the night frosts never come near.

This applies particularly to the smallest of the two Titian-red
calves. In fact, it's the littlest of the lot and must have left its mother

at a very early age.

The little calf gets tired very easily, chiefly, I believe, because of its long journey from Oban.

Drumbuie understands completely and waits patiently, ensuring the others do, too, when the "wee one" flops down.

Drumbuie really does care about the baby of his family and, besides, there is the bonus of being able to rest his old bones whilst "baby-sitting!"

All of which leaves us no choice but to christen the tiny red calf "The Bairn", and the bigger one Ruaraidh, or "Red One".

Then there are the two calves from Coll.

They have rarely seen human beings before, but show no signs of nervousness at my approach and will stand quite still while I scratch between their shoulder blades.

It's such a wonderful feeling to win the confidence of any animal born to be wild and free.

Those two calves are so different from the others.

They have long, silky coats that have a silvery, oyster-shell sheen with just a hint of a soft, dark underlay.

That's probably because their father was a black bull, the original colour of the Highland cattle.

Coll, their former home, is a small island lying far out to sea with its shores lapped on all sides by the Atlantic Ocean.

That's a long way from Croft Douglas, but the calves really seem to like it here and we have named one Dileas, "Faithful," because it has stayed by Drumbuie's side from the moment of meeting him.

The other is called Dorcha, "Darker One."

I have left little Buie, "The Golden One," to the end because I think he is something special.

I don't have to go to see him - he comes running, with his golden hair flying, to meet me!

He is so full of fun, but kindly, gentle and thoughtful, too, bringing sunshine, with his glinting coat, wherever he goes.

When we meet, his soft, moist nose "wuffles" a stream of warm

155

words into my ear, all about being so pleased to see me and, in return, he gets a rewarding tickle in all the places he can't reach.

Then he lovingly licks my hand with his tiny pink tongue before I go.

The sun is high in the heavens and it's not really a day now for doing anything that isn't absolutely necessary.

So, instead of weeding the garden, I sit down and watch a bunch of groundsel releasing a series of seeds.

The head of a groundsel flower has lots of seeds, each one with a light, white, silky parachute of its own, which drifts away to the will of a wayward wind, hoping to land on some fertile ground and germinate.

Groundsel can be a bit of a nuisance to gardeners, but a boon to the birds, so this bunch has been purposefully left with the birds in mind.

There are some already watching the parachuting groundsel seeds. It's a family of goldfinches, perched in a row on the long branch of a rose bush.

We don't usually get goldfinches in this part of the Highlands until the autumn when all the thistle seeds are ripe.

This pair must have nested here because they have five little ones!

Goldfinches are the smallest of the finch family, and are dainty, colourful birds.

The male and female make such a loving couple - and, even beyond their courting and nest-building, when they have a large family to look after, still find time to exchange tender beak-to-beak kisses.

Looking at them now, it's no wonder to me that the family group is called a "charm".

I was working far away from home on my seventeenth birthday, when the postman brought me a five pound note from my dad, who never did anything by halves, regardless of his financial position.

Five pounds represented a lot of money at that time and there were so many things that I wanted, but they all got blown away, like the groundsel seeds in the wind, when I saw a man crouched in a circle of whin bushes aglow with yellow blooms.

He stood up as I approached and must have been well over six feet tall.

His big, barrel chest made him look, as they say, as broad as he was long, and a very rough-looking character, too, with a pair of piercing black eyes set in a furtive face.

"What," I said, "are you going to do with these?" pointing to a large cage where a bunch of goldfinches were beating their wings and bodies wildly against its wire bars.

"Sell 'em, of course," he replied. "They will fetch a pound of two."

I produced the crisp five pound note from my pocket and inquired, "Will that buy them?"

The big man showed a row of yellow teeth under his red moustache and said, "That will do."

"That one too," I insisted, pointing to a tiny cage on top of the whin bushes, containing a cock goldfinch that kept singing a sweet, tuneful song.

"No fear!" the big man growled fiercely, picking up his stick again. "That's my decoy. I can't catch any more without him."

But, with my heart pounding, I stood my ground and said I had paid for all the goldfinches and if I didn't get them I would report him to the police.

The big man took a menacing step towards me then, snarled and slunk away.

It felt so good to watch the charm of caged goldfinches fly free again and I felt sure Dad would be proud of what I had bought with his birthday present.

Do Not Forsake Me

A "Viking invasion" affects everyone at Croft Douglas, while Gideon recalls how a matter of life and death led to a change of heart...

Most houses in the Highlands have a robin flitting around the front door at this time of year when food is hard to find.

These colourful little birds are family favourites everywhere and it's no wonder they're picked to appear on countless thousands of greeting cards.

But they have other attributes and I, for one, am still learning a lot about them.

Not so long ago people thought the robin's mate was the pert, pretty little Jenny Wren, while others believed that only the cock bird has a red breast because hen birds wear more sombre plumage as a camouflage to conceal them from predators.

It has been established, however, that in the robin's case, both birds have almost identical plumage.

Robins are very territorially minded and a pair will choose what they believe to be an ideal place to set up home, like a vegetable garden where the soil and the plants will provide plenty of feeding and, when the time comes, a nesting site.

Alternatively, a sheltered hedgerow with its share of foodstuffs, under a grassy bank beside a rippling burn, or in an orchard where the fruit trees attract a host of insects, are also places to be seriously considered.

The robins can be very aggressive little birds and defend a chosen territory by flashing their red breasts and fiercely driving off any would-be settlers if they won't heed the warning.

However, we do have one exception here - a migrant relative from a faraway land who takes over the garden in front of our house when he arrives.

That's when our robins forget about flaunting their fiery breasts and, apparently deciding that discretion is the better part of valour, retire to the vegetable garden.

The migrant is a bold and fearless bird who seems, to me, to be somewhat bigger than our garden birds, with a very prominent white "vee" dividing his red breast.

I'm sure it stands for "Viking", so that's what I call him.

It's not all doom and gloom for the garden robins, however.

Their distant cousin, from somewhere in Scandinavia, proves to be a feathered life insurance policy when predators, like sparrowhawks, make regular daylight raids on the garden, swooping down from the sky to strike like lightning.

But The Viking rises bravely to meet them, putting the hawks completely off balance and leaving them clutching only thin air with their outstretched claws.

This gives the garden robins time to seek shelter until the frustrated predator has flown away.

First thing in the morning, The Viking is waiting impatiently at the kitchen window, tapping on the glass from time to time for a piece of warm toast, which he helps himself to from my hand.

A little later, when I take a tray of kitchen scraps to the hens, this mighty atom meets me at the porch, perches on the tray and picks out the tastiest pieces!

The amount of food that this little robin manages to stuff into such a small body absolutely astonishes me, but he is sensibly "stoking up" so that his body can withstand the freezing cold of the nights to come.

Seumas, a shepherd on the south side of Loch Tummel, owned a huge flock of blackface sheep that roamed the hills from Schiehallion in the West to Creag-an-loch in the East.

He had his elder son to help him with the shepherding but his young son, Jamie, had just left school and presented a problem.

There was only one available job for Jamie - driving away the hares from their homes in the mountains and making room for more sheep, so they could eat the sweet, succulent heather tips that were the favourite food of the hares.

So Seumas called on all the farmers and shepherds to help and, one morning early in the New Year, they all met on the shoulder of Schiehallion, the hill of the fairies.

Jamie, for whose benefit all this had been arranged, was more than reluctant to be any part of the hare drive because he had a great love for all animals, and saw that most of the men were carrying guns.

But his father was insistent, so Jamie took only a hazel stick, then fell in line with the rest.

They moved off at a given signal, with a warning not to lose sight of the person next to them.

It wasn't really a day to be on the mountain tops, with danger lurking on the icy crags and in the deep snow.

Worse still, before long a dense mist suddenly descended and Jamie, although he shouted and shouted, found himself all alone.

He could just see the black, velvety tips on the ears of a white hare that loped in front of him and he decided to follow it. But, before he had gone very far, his feet went through a sheet of snow and ice into a peat bog below.

No matter how much Jamie struggled, he couldn't free himself from the bog's cold, clammy clutches.

As the mist slowly lifted, he saw a little wraith-like form which seemed to be beckoning him.

With a supreme effort, Jamie clawed his way out of the bog and crawled behind the flitting figure to find himself in a small cave where he collapsed onto a bed of dry bracken.

Everyone except Jamie had reported back to the rendezvous point at Foss Farmhouse, so a search party was immediately sent out as darkness was falling.

The bright beams of their torches danced like fireflies in the snow.

No-one needed to be told how vital it was to find Jamie as soon as possible on this bitterly cold night, with a snow blizzard building up threateningly in the West.

Suddenly a shot shattered the silence of the night. It was a signal that someone had found him, curled up in the little cave.

Jamie said later that he felt sure it was a white hare that had shown him where to shelter. So, from that day to this, there has been no more talk of driving the hares from the hilltops.

Shortly afterwards, Jamie left home and won his way to a managerial position in a large agricultural company.

But I can't help wondering if it was a white hare that saved Jamie's life, or one of the world-famous Schiehallion fairies...

Starting Over

*While the cattle make the most of the sumptuous spread
Nature has laid out before them, some seasoned travellers
are finally on the home straight...*

It's always so wonderful to witness the yearly miracle of spring
moving rhythmically into summer and the regeneration of plant
and animal life.

It's also wonderful to know that, for the following six months,
there will be an abundance of sweet, green grass and herbage.

This is the finest of food for our Highland cattle, those hardy,
longhorned, hairy beasties who live their lives outside in all kinds
of weather and will not now need any form of supplementary
feeding for as long as this lush feast lasts.

The cattle feed mostly in the cool of the evening and in the early
morning during the long, light summer days when the sun can only
"catnap", and night-time is just a few short shadows.

Then, with full tummies, they will select a suitable spot to lie
down and sleep, or contentedly chew the cud during the heat of the
day.

But when there is a cool breeze blowing, the cattle will climb
the banks and braes and come up from the lochside to keep us
company.

They lie around the farm buildings, admiring the heavenly view
for hours on end, with the warmth of the sun on their backs and the
light west wind fanning their faces.

That's usually the time when my daughter Shona takes the
opportunity to indulge in some beautifying teasing technique,
selecting the Highlanders she thinks are in most need of a grooming

session.

Drumbuie, our big bull, comes in for the most attention.

He is usually the last to cast his long winter coat of hair, because of the large area of his body.

He is also so appreciative of having help with all the places he can't reach with the point of his horn, particularly the patches of old matted hair he can do nothing with.

Shona removes these with the expertise of a surgeon. Her reward is in seeing how handsome the big bull looks with his brand-new silky summer coat, now gleaming like russet-red satin in the sunshine.

Then Shona adds the finishing touch by brushing and teasing out the Titian tassel that floats through the air like a copper-coloured cloud every time he switches his tail.

Salmon, although born and bred in fresh water, spend most of their lives at sea.

Those returning now for the first time, we call "grilse".

It's not really known how the grilse, after travelling thousands of miles, find their way back to where they were born, but it's firmly believed that they follow the smell of the water flowing from their birthplace, welcoming them home.

This is the time, too, when the countless "darling buds" of wild roses begin to bloom in a riot of colour along the riverbanks.

I'm sure the young, homecoming salmon can smell their exotic perfume, too!

Drumbuie certainly does, but never touches the flowers until they have shed their petals and, even then, waits until weeks later, when the fruit of the wild rose starts to ripen.

This is an annual feast for the birds of the air and the beasts of the field.

Drumbuie drools over every mouthful of the luscious, rosy-red hips, packed to bursting point with concentrated Vitamin C.

I am quite convinced that they have helped to keep my beloved big bull looking ridiculously young in his advancing years.

The people who specialise in going "Down Your Way" come

up for a change, to the Highlands.

Drumbuie, of course, became the centre of attraction and, taking full advantage of these moments, showed off shamelessly.

So much so that, in no time at all, the entire team were thoroughly convinced that this ton-weight of hairy Highland bone and muscle, topped off with a five-foot spread of huge horns that would have frightened the life out of any Spanish matador was, after all, just a soft-hearted, hairy teddy bear longing to be tickled and cuddled!

How on earth, I asked myself, do you follow an act like that?

I should have known better, for don't they always say, "Never appear with animals or children"?

However, I did my best and found the easiest question to answer was the final one.

"What record would you like played at the end of the programme?"

I just love listening to the soothing, expressive piece of music that persuades me to take a stroll with my soul, "Wild Roses" by Franz Lehar.

The Young One

*There's sadness in the air as the majestic mountains don
their misty winter garb and Gideon and Irralee mourn the
loss of a dear departed friend...*

How moody the hills have been this month. They always seem
to feel their age when the year itself is growing old, and sometimes
turbulent tremors shake their huge shoulders as if each of them is
thinking about something they just can't share.

It's then they withdraw secretly from one another to hide under
clammy clouds of mist that they wrap in ever-increasing folds
around their rugged figures. This only serves to make them appear
more miserable still.

It always seems such a sad day when the hills fall out, because,
after all, they are next-door neighbours and no-one ever knows
when they may need help from a neighbour.

I think it has something to do with the loss of their regal purple
robes which they won't regain until next summer. In the meantime
they have to make do with the dull, wintry wear that, worse still,
is now powdered with the first fall of snow.

The mountain sitting serenely at the top of the loch always
seems to have the least to say, possibly because it's the only one
with a volcanic voice, and has the deepest respect of all the
surrounding hills, great and small.

But Schiehallion, with its all-powerful armament, still seeks a
peaceful solution and has more than a little influence over the
elements.

With a diplomatic approach it makes orders seem like requests,
and appeals to the south-west wind to mop up there misery-

spreading mists as silently as possible.

In no time at all the clinging, low-lying clouds are swept in shredded rolls up the rugged hillsides to disappear into a duck-egg blue sky and allow a watery sun to distribute some warm blinks of sunshine to make the hills happy and friendly again.

Irralee had such high hopes for her snow-white Samoyed dog, Hercules. His first successes in the show-ring had her over the moon but, alas, all her carefully-laid plans for the future of handsome Hercules were swept away and lost, like snowflakes in a fast-flowing river, when he developed internal trouble and, despite her hopes for his recovery, he only survived the necessary operation for a short hour or two.

A happening such as this causes such a hurt inside me that I am like a wounded animal whose only wish is to hide until all is healed.

Irralee is made of different material and much more practical. She does have a good cry, but then quickly brushes away the debris of her tears and does something constructive, like searching for another Samoyed puppy, and Irralee, when she is looking for something that really matters, leaves no stone unturned.

She finally heard of a lady in Edinburgh who had a very young pup whose father is at present seeking his first championship in the show-ring. His name was a spectacular one, Hurkur Heartthrob.

How, I thought, could anything go wrong with a puppy who was the progeny of a Heartthrob!

Irralee brought this small, animated snowball to Croft Douglas where she was immediately christened Herka with a splash of special water from the wishing well and introduced to Ceilidh, my little spotted Spaniel, who was so excited at being given charge of a snow-white puppy she could call her own.

Herka, who by now must have been missing her won mother, decided that Ceilidh's soft, silky, spotted side, so full of warmth and motherliness was the best place to be, cuddled in and fell fast asleep.

Ceilidh, although fully aware that she was going to miss a meal, didn't dare move a muscle for fear of waking the little one.

How she lives for, and loves to look after, puppies, beginning by pretending that they are her very own and ending up believing they really are! I am convinced that this is what keeps Ceilidh looking so young.

She also saw to it that Herka's education started as soon as possible, by sitting absolutely still and saying some sort of canine grace before commencing a meal.

She also seems to be of the considered opinion that every well-bred puppy should be taught, as she was, to fetch and carry properly, starting with the transport of her beloved bone.

Herka proves to be a more than apt pupil and after Ceilidh has given a demonstration of how the carrying of a bone is done correctly, Herka just can't wait to get to grips with the treasured object herself.

They are both so different in build and temperament, Ceilidh always seeks a warm, sunny spot for a relaxing sleep, but the sun is in short supply at this time of year, only doing a very short circuit across the sky.

So Ceilidh has to settle for a seat beside the glowing log fire, wriggling appreciatively whilst the warmth creeps through her silky skin.

Herka, on the other hand, can't stand the heat and loves to lie on the cool stone slab that serves as our front doorstep and gaze at the stars.

Tonight I'm listening to a sweet sound I haven't heard for some time. It's the sound of a woman singing softly to herself, and a sure sign that, once again, everything is well with Irralee's world.

Bridge Over Troubled Waters

*Emergency measures are called for when a vital member of
the community becomes a liability, while Gideon remains
ever-optimistic that an old friend will pay a return visit...*

There's a lady reader from Port Elizabeth who has the kind
thought of sending me a postcard every month. The one I am now
holding in my hand gently reminds me that summer has come to
South Africa, so winter must be almost with us, here in the
Highlands.

All the signs, weather and wildlife-wise, say winter can't be far
away, with robins bob-bobbing about everywhere, skirling their
cheerful, tuneful little songs.

For weeks now the trees have been all dressed up in a galaxy of
colour, one of the most breathtaking sights being the Pass of
Killiecrankie, which looks at its best from the bridge spanning the
River Garry.

Before this bridge was built, the main link to the Strathtummel
road was over one of the narrowest places on the Garry Gorge by
means of a "Bailey bridge", built by Army Engineers as an
exercise.

They must have been very proud of their project and, when
completed, put a plaque on its stout iron framework to say so.

It was a credit to the Army Engineers' handiwork that the
Bailey bridge clung for so long, if somewhat precariously, to each
rocky side of the gorge, when it could have been forgiven for
collapsing a long time ago.

But erosion was clawing its destructive, crumbling way along
the rocky ledges supporting the bridge on either side, making the

entire structure downright dangerous.

Being on the local Education Committee at the time, I fought hard to have a brand-new bridge built, but only received some vague, half-hearted promises about what might happen in the future.

Worse was to follow when, one morning, Irralee set off in the car to do some shopping in Pitlochry.

As she approached the old bridge, she spotted a bunch of men working underneath and at the sides of the bridge, trying to reinforce its grip on the rocks, where a pattern of huge cracks had appeared.

Irralee mistook the workmen's frantic warning waves to stop as merely friendly ones, waved merrily back and sped over the rickety, rackety old bridge, wondering why it was so noisy!

When she eventually reached the other side, without having plunged down the gorge into the turbulent waters of the Garry, the workmen heaved a huge sigh of relief.

Then, before proceeding with any more emergency repairs, they barricaded both entrances to the bridge, leaving Irralee with the dubious distinction of being the last person to cross, after the Bailey bridge had been pronounced "dangerous in the extreme."

Repairs to strengthen the supports on either side of the bridge took some considerable time, for as the old Highland saying goes, "There's no hurry north of Dunkeld."

In the meantime the school bus, all cars and people on foot had to halt at the closed bridge and make a long detour by the single track Tenandry road to Killiecrankie, before being able to reach the road to Pitlochry.

The only person who was pleased about this roundabout journey was the minister, whose church and manse were settled comfortably at the side of this road. He was heard to remark that God moved in mysterious ways, for the bridge repairs had given him the opportunity to meet some parishioners he hadn't seen for years!

The bridge was finally patched and, unceremoniously, declared open, although it now carried a prominent warning notice, limiting the weight of vehicles wishing to cross.

This restriction caused me to worry about the varying weight of the school bus and, more importantly, the precious cargo of children it was carrying.

Yet all my efforts to alert the Education Authority were to no avail and only met with a series of shaking heads and endless excuses about being unable to afford the expense incurred.

Thankfully, a solution to the problem came suddenly in the unlikely shape of a General Election. This was something that the folk of the bens and the glens really savoured.

Attending all the party political meetings with the opportunity of heckling a would-be MP was great entertainment, second only to a good-going ceilidh!

So, on this occasion they flocked to the Kinloch Rannoch Hall to hear Sir Alec Douglas-Home speaking in a bid to win this safe Highland seat.

I arrived early, but the hall was already packed to suffocation.

The stewards on the doors, who resembled all-in wrestlers, tried to turn me away but, when a lady left saying she felt slightly sick, I brightly suggested to the "musclemen" that there must be a seat now.

They surveyed me critically, seemingly unsure of my political leanings, but eventually ushered me to an easily accessible seat at the end of a row.

I took this stroke of luck to be an omen that I was meant to attend the meeting.

When "Question Time", the main event of the evening, was being announced, I had the feeling that lots of local worthies were here, primed with specially prepared "awkward" questions.

But before they could challenge our would-be MP, I got off to a flying start by jumping to my feet and making a passionate plea for a new bridge across the gorge of the River Garry, so that everybody, and especially the bus crowded with schoolchildren, could cross safely.

Sir Alex exchanged some hurried whispers with local party members supporting him on the platform, then he broke the silence by solemnly announcing, "If I am elected, this bridge will be built immediately."

The hall erupted as the cheering crowd chanted, "Home rule for the Highlands!"

Sir Alec was duly elected and was as good as his word.

Now, whenever I cross the River Garry, I like to feel that a wee, wee bit of this magnificent new bridge belongs to me.

There as so many red-breasted robins about at this time of year, because they are mainly migrants from other countries who have come to spend the winter with us.

My favourite, never-to-be-forgotten, ever-so-friendly robin came to Croft Douglas two winters in succession.

He was fearless, with a heart far bigger than his body, and flew in the face of s striking sparrowhawk to save a tiny blue tit.

This dynamic robin had a distinctive white "vee" that divided his fiery breast feathers, and he always flitted faithfully around my head and followed me everywhere.

I called him "The Viking."

He didn't come back last winter, but at this time of year, I still keep a yearning, longing look-out for a friendly robin wearing a big white vee on his red breast - just like The Viking.

Handle With Care!

When the golden broom blooms are flourishing, there's trouble afoot when the unfortunate Drumbuie comes a cropper and giving a helping hand proves to be easier said than done.

When the broom blooms in the Highlands, it turns the roadsides into broad pathways bordered with gold, and brings a blaze of sunshine to the dullest day.

The broom bush has such a beautiful flower, but no sweet nectar to offer as hospitality for a honey bee.

The bee knows this full well but he is a worker and, feeling entitled to some time off, takes the opportunity to spend a pleasant moment or two visiting the broom blooms, just for the sheer pleasure of embracing the exotic golden flowers.

This is just what the broom had hoped and planned for.

The caress of the honey bee on the petals triggers off a tiny explosive device that dusts the bee with pollen and fills him with the desire to visit a neighbouring flower...and yet another!

So pollination is completed and the future of the broom is assured.

A bear with a sore head pales into insignificance compared to a big hairy Highland bull, weighing well over a ton, with a wound in his foot.

Those were my thoughts this morning as Drumbuie limped towards me trailing his hind leg and looking an abject picture of misery.

When I approached him he signalled, in no uncertain manner, that this was not a moment to come anywhere near, by weaving his huge span of horns from side to side and, from time to time, thrashing his head against the leg that was causing him so much trouble.

This is when I say to myself, "Well, why don't you keep a hamster instead of a Highland bull? It would be so much easier to handle if it needed the attention of a veterinary surgeon."

And I knew instinctively that Drumbuie now needed just that and quickly phoned for professional help.

It took more than a bit of time to coax my big bull into the catching pen, and I suffered with him as he painfully limped every long, tortuous step of the way.

But I couldn't possibly get him into the final confining compartment that has stout corner posts embedded in concrete, because Drumbuie's horns are now far too big to negotiate the narrow entrance.

By this time the vet had arrived.

I could see his car pulling up at the side of the house and hoped fervently that he wasn't the one who had been "done over" by a bull before, and who therefore would insist that Drumbuie was safely and properly secured before he started his examination.

But this is just a young fellow who can't be so long out of school. He must be the new junior partner who has just joined the local firm of vets.

When I tried to explain that I can't get my big bull a step further than the lead-in pen where he has more than a bit of room to manoeuvre, I felt that many a battle-scarred veteran of the veterinary brigade would have backed away at that moment.

But the young man advanced, with the stamp of confidence in his step.

Inwardly, I worried about him, thinking, Is this his first assignment outside the pets' surgery?

But in the next moment or two I wondered what I had been worrying about when the young vet commenced his examination in a calm and collected fashion.

He finished by saying. "I'll have to lift his foot and have a look."

This was when I felt that my worst fears could be confirmed.

Whilst I was sure that Drumbuie knew we were only trying to help him, he had never had his foot lifted by human hand in his life!

He was unconfined, without even a halter, and could use and move his ton weight any way he wanted to!

So I put all of my ten-and-a-half stone against his broad backside to brace his good hind leg, dug my fingernails into the root of his tail and scrubbed feverishly, because this is the out-of-reach spot he loves to be scratched.

I then offered up a silent prayer and, with a nod of my head, indicated to the young vet that this was the moment.

I am now completely convinced in the power of prayer, coupled with a wealth of understanding on the young vet's part, as he lifted Drumbuie's injured leg and spoke some soothing words like, "This won't take long and you wouldn't kick me old boy, would you?"

Then, like a blacksmith about to shoe a horse, he tucked Drumbuie's hoof between his legs and, with something that resembled a surgeon's scalpel, went to work.

This gave me a moment to remember the lady who has recently written to me wondering if Drumbuie was real, and I mentally composed my reply.

Meantime, the young vet had completed his excavations and triumphantly announced, "Ah, here's a hole in the hoof and it's infected."

Brushing aside my anxious inquiries, he added, "Not to worry, we'll soon fix that. I'll just have to give him a jag."

I braced myself as the vet placed the nozzle of the needle in my big bull's broad back and suffered, too, when the flat of his hand slammed it home into the thick hide.

But dear old Drumbuie didn't move a muscle and when the vet pumped a flow of antibiotics into his bloodstream, he seemed to know that he would sleep peacefully tonight.

I have learned to duck, instinctively, when Drumbuie suddenly swings his head round, but on this occasion I was a perfect target for his long, warm tongue that wrapped itself lovingly around my face.

The young vet handed me a packet of powders as he climbed back into his car saying, "One morning and night for the next six days," and then he was gone before I could ask him, "How?"

So I hollowed out a potato, put the powder in, and offered it to Drumbuie - who promptly spat it out!

I suspected the powder had a bitter taste, so I topped the next potato up with treacle.

Drumbuie drooled over it and assured me it was delicious.

I've just had a charming letter from the lady who'd written before, saying she was so glad Drumbuie had fully recovered from his injury and that he was real!

There's an old country saying that, when gorse is out of bloom, kissing is out of fashion.

Gorse is called whin in Scotland, and we have only one tiny bush on the hill, which runs out of bloom by the end of July.

Irralee says she has seen whin in full bloom as late as October, near the New Forest.

"What about kissing in Scotland when the whin blooms only in summer?" I asked.

"Scots lovers," Irralee assured me, "will know how to keep themselves warm without the aid of whin blooming."

I ventured to suggest that I had been talking not about warmth, but kissing.

Irralee looked at me as if I were some small boy in need of enlightenment and, with a sigh, said, "A soft, warm, understanding word, that someone wants so much to hear, is a kiss to the heart."

Homeward Bound

*Gideon recalls how daughter Maureen, a happy-go-lucky
girl with some very special playmates, bravely faced up to
adversity and found a new lease of life...*

Just like the silvery salmon swims back hundreds of hazardous
miles to the hill burn where it was born, or the swallow with an
inbuilt navigation system, second to none, flies halfway across the
world to reach the roof of a barn in the Highlands and the nest it was
reared in as a fledgling, Maureen, our eldest daughter, comes back
to Croft Douglas whenever she feels the need.

I remember so well when Maureen was just a chubby little
toddler who loved to wander about the croft with her big teddy bear
dangling from one hand, bump-bumping along behind her.

How happy she was with plenty to time to talk to the flowers
and say "thank you" to the thrushes, chaffinches and willow
warblers who, she was sure, sang the sweetest songs especially for
her.

When she found a bee sipping nectar from the heart of a flower,
she would carefully wrap her tiny handkerchief around the bloom
then, clasping it close to the stem, she'd kneel down and listen with
bated breath to the song of the bumble bee, a confidential buzzing
containing so many secrets that Maureen was convinced were for
her ears alone.

Then, like a magician, she swept her hankie away, to reveal this
beautiful bee as it took off like a Hercules transport aircraft,
heavily laden with pollen for honey. Humming a friendly farewell
song, it circled slowly round Maureen's head before flying off to
its secret honey store.

This was an old woodpecker's nest in an oak tree down by the lochside that the bumble bee had already told her all about.

One day we heard little Maureen crying her heart out in the middle of our herd of Highland cattle.

Irralee and I both felt that something must be desperately wrong, because those big gentle-hearted, hairy beasts would never harm a defenceless little one.

We found Maureen standing in front of the big bull, pointing a chubby finger accusingly at him and sobbing because he was standing on a pretty bunch of yellow primroses!

How he hung his head in shame.

Whilst in her early teens, Maureen was struck by a mysterious internal trouble and taken to Perth for "tests and observation."

All this took some considerable time and countless long journeys to make sure that someone was always there at the visiting hours.

Surely this can't last much longer, we thought, but Maureen's fifteenth birthday was celebrated in Perth Royal Infirmary and I staggered up the stairs to her ward with a big cake specially baked for the occasion.

Irralee was right behind me with her present, a battery-powered record player that, at the press of a button, produced Maureen's favourite song of the moment, "I Remember you."

The journeys became longer still when Maureen was moved to Edinburgh, where a specialist solemnly assured me she was in urgent need of major surgery, for which I would be required to sign.

In that moment, it seemed so wrong to me that this could all be happening to one so young.

When I was allowed to see Maureen, the nurse whispered to me beforehand, "If you feel disturbed, don't let on."

Disturbed! I was devastated by the sight of my daughter lying so still, connected to a series of plastic tubes, whilst a huge drip bag hung overhead like some ghostly apparition.

The card placed prominently at the head of the bed read, in bold, black letters, "Sips of water only."

I had to tell myself repeatedly when I felt my knees buckling, "You're a fellow and not supposed to faint."

I was eventually rewarded by the glint of recognition in Maureen's eyes as they fluttered open and the warm grip of her hand which wordlessly said, "I'm so glad you're here."

That worked wonders for me, and the tight knot in my tummy gradually unwound itself.

My niece, Lesley, is a fun-loving girl with a freckled face that's so easy to look at. She shares the belief of her husband, George, that helping humanity is the best possible passport to Heaven.

So George had a casual word with his friend Bob, a handsome young heating engineer, suggesting that he should visit Maureen, who had suffered so much, and help to brighten her day.

Bob did more than that, sending a note to say he was coming and enclosing a photograph taken in his football strip while playing for an Edinburgh club.

Maureen was over the moon when she received his letter and brightened up immediately.

The nurses detected the difference right away and, on gaining the privilege of a peep at the special letter, aided and abetted Maureen in every way to prepare her for her visitor.

She was bed-bathed, perfumed and her blonde hair slicked into golden sausage curls and harnessed with pink ribbons, finishing with just a suggestion of sky-blue eyeshadow and an ever-so-slight lick of lipstick.

Just a second before the double doors were opened to release a waiting wave of visitors that swept down the ward, Maureen tucked her legs tightly underneath herself to control her excitement.

She recognised Bob immediately from his photograph as he shyly advanced clutching a massive bouquet of flowers.

They talked of this and that and Maureen, feeling more relaxed, unleashed her legs and slid them down the bed.

Whereupon Bob gave a gigantic gasp of relief and, clutching Maureen's hand, confessed, "At first I thought you had no legs!"

The nurses, who were so excited about Maureen's visitor, were hovering about nearby and heard Bob's confession, which simply sent them into stitches.

By this time Maureen and Bob were chuckling, too, and the laughter rippled throughout the ward as everyone joined in the merriment.

Maureen is staying with us this weekend because her husband, Bob, is sorting out technical problems in Brighton.

She has survived seven operations and now looks the picture of health.

We have two motherless lambs, reared in the collie dogs' kennel run, and it's now time for them to join a neighbour's flock and mix with their own kind.

Who better than Maureen to give the little lambs a reassuring cuddle before they go, just to put them in the picture about facing up to the trials of life. Because if anyone knows what plucking up courage is all about, she does.

The Long Journey

Gideon worries about some late starters, while Irralee is in for a shock when she returns home!

We were really worried this year when it was time for all the swallows to gather together and go to a warmer climate for the winter.

The birds who nested on the high wooden beams in the barn and had successfully brought up a family of four, had decided to rear another brood, with the result that the latest little swallows were still peeping over the edge of the nest when their older brothers and sisters were all ready to "take off" on the first, and longest, flight of their lives.

It was then that the parent birds appeared to make an important decision, that one would go with the first family, while the other stayed on, to follow later when the second brood of babes was strong enough.

It must have been a touching moment when the parents parted and one swallow watched its mate fly away into the blue, with the first born. This could have caused them both a bit of heartache, but the cock bird, who had elected to stay, certainly didn't show it, and got busy stuffing as much food as he could catch into the four remaining open mouths.

I shared his anxiety that the weather could, at any time, become much crisper and colder, bringing white frosts early to make insect food more than hard to find. So the senior swallow worked tirelessly, knowing full well that these young birds must build an extra layer of fat on their bodies, a sort of extra "flight fuel" before being fit to travel so far.

I got to know the cheery, chubby, little faces of those four baby swallows as they peered down at me over the rim round their nest. They were so well "brought up" and their manners impeccable, with no quarrelling, purposeful jostling or pushing as they grew stronger, so no-one would be forced to leave the nest before being perfectly prepared to do so!

This is unlike some other fledglings who, when they become almost fully feathered, flutter and flop from the nest, flitting uncertainly a lot sooner than they should and generally being a great source of anxiety to their parents.

Young swallows, though, with their long, strong, flight feathers fully developed, are ready to reach for the sky as soon as they leave their nest. That's when my four "late little ones," with two weeks of patient waiting without any undue movement, really let go!

They didn't seem to give a second's thought to such mundane things as finding food for themselves, but spent their first few hours in space, seeing which one of them could fly the fastest, vying with each other to see who could make the most spectacular twists and turns then, with daring speed, diving earthwards, wingtip to wingtip, almost brushing the ground before, effortlessly, turning together to zoom upwards like an arrow streaking to the top of the blue sky, swiftly returning for yet another intricate aerial game.

What fun they had together with the joy of starting out on life's great adventure. It was almost as if they knew that, next morning, they would be called to assemble on the barn roof, sit silently in line and listen to the cock bird telling them, in a series of twitterings, just exactly why, and where, they were going and what they had to do.

And sure enough, one fine crisp September morning I saw the four young swallows fly away in formation.

It was a moment tinged with sadness.

"They'll be all right," I told myself, "with their father to look after them and I'm sure he also has an assignment with his lovely little wife in some sunny spot somewhere."

Sandy is a Highland telephone engineer and has lots of travelling to do in his hardy all-weather transport, with the responsibility of ensuring that all the telephone installations in his territory around the bens and glens are in perfect working order.

This can be a vital, life-saving task during the wild winter weeks, when bitter, biting winds blow across the Highland moors like wild, unbridled horses and, worse still, often bring a blinding, blizzarding snowstorm with them.

This results in a "white out" that tenders roads impassable and hard to find. It also used to play havoc with telegraph poles and the lines of communication but, happily, that's one problem that has now been solved, by simply putting the wires, in cable form, underground.

Sandy has, however, an even more distinctive part to play in life as Pipe Major of The Atholl Highlanders Pipe Band, leading the world-famous Duke of Atholl's Private Army, an honour presented to the Duke by Queen Victoria.

To see the Atholl Highlanders on parade is truly a magnificent, colourful, awe-inspiring, sight.

As one famous English General, after reviewing a Highland Regiment, is credited with saying, "If there has to be a battle, let them lead the attack. They are bound to give the enemy a big fright because, By Golly, they frighten me!"

Sandy is a piper plus and one I have frequently taken with me whilst promoting Highland holidays, chiefly in Scandinavia and Germany for the Scottish Tourist Board's big brother, the British Tourist Association.

But, on this particular occasion, it was the special request of a foreign camera crew for models wearing Scottish tartans and woollens, using the heathery Croft Douglas hill as a background.

There was also something different about this film company - they were all ladies, including the "camera man."

They also required a piper to take part. Sandy was more than delighted to oblige.

I told the models they could change their clothes in the house as there was no-one else around, but had completely forgotten to tell Irralee that the film company was coming!

She returned early from a visit to Perth to find the girls, in various stages of undress, in the living-room whilst I was still with Sandy on the hill.

Fortunately, the director diplomatically chose that moment to present Irralee with a huge box of Continental chocolates!

As I turn out the light tonight, I wonder where our swallows are now.

I know they can cleverly navigate by the sun during daylight and the stars at night, on their long journey first to the south of England, across the Channel to fly over France, then Spain, crossing water again when they come to the Mediterranean, wending their way through sunny Africa to a well-earned rest south of the Sahara.

Tonight I send them a special, heartfelt wish in Gaelic, to keep them safe.

"Beannachd leibh" - Blessings are with you.

Our Hero!

*A newcomer to the Strath has an uphill struggle ahead of
him, but a little faith and a lot of elbow grease mean he's
soon something of a local hero...*

Sometimes, even at this time year, we have to wait until the
snowplough, with its gyrating, mechanical gritter, goes growling
past before venturing out on to a snowbound or treacherously icy
road.

It can be quite late in the day before our road is clear because
the snowplough has had priority work to do on the big main roads.

And yet, not so long ago, we used to have the luxury of our own
"resident roadman" who kept the stretch of Strathtummel road in
first-class condition, and had a house that went with the job.

He was from the Isles - not a big man, but he had a muscular
build that was something between a weightlifter and a long-
distance runner, and he was so proud of every winding mile under
his charge.

When we first met I introduced myself and enquired his name,
whereupon our Island roadman straightened smartly to attention
and announced, "I'm MacLeod of MacLeod."

This intrigued me, as I thought a title of this nature usually
belonged to a Highland chieftain, or someone of that ilk.

So, with great daring, I went further and asked, "Why `of
MacLeod'?"

Our roadman reverently raised his face, with its finely chiselled
cheekbones, to the sky and said, "Because my father was a
MacLeod."

There was just no answer to that, but he seemed to be expecting another question so, deciding not to disappoint him, I enquired as to the nature of his first name.

MacLeod's features lit up and I knew, in that moment, I had scored a "bull's-eye".

He was gasping to tell me and proudly announced, "It's Peregrine!"

He must have been delighted with my reaction, for this, in my experience, was a name reserved by the highly born for the eldest son.

Not only that, but MacLeod did look extremely like a falcon with his long, aristocratically hooked nose and piercing eyes.

I ventured still further and, with bated breath, delivered my final question: "Was your father a chieftain?"

MacLeod reached out and wrung my hand with a vice-like grip. "Yes, yes," he assured me. "My father was chief roadman of the Island."

My heart warmed to MacLeod because I thought, just like he did, that my father ranked with the highest in the world - a Prince among men.

We soon discovered something else - our new roadman on the Road to the Isles was not only "highly born" but one of the best in the business.

Long before the dawn was drawing its first thin pencil line of early light across the sky at the east end of Loch Tummel, MacLeod left the warmth of his bed on many a freezing cold morning and quick-marched a mile or more to reach the Allean Brae.

This is a steep, winding hill that leads to the world-famous Queen's View which, because she thought it breathtaking, Victoria named after herself.

The vehicle that concerned MacLeod the most on these mornings was the school bus, packed full of children picked up at intervals all the way from Kinloch Rannoch to Pitlochry.

It was due at twenty minutes past eight and it was MacLeod's responsibility that Allean Brae was safe to travel by that time.

He quickly demolished the snowdrifts that stretched from one side of the road to the other with his trusty shovel.

Then, working like a Trojan, he spread every yard of the winding road with grit dug from the piles of gravel he had previously placed there.

He had always finished his task before the school bus came and, by this time, had taken his jacket, shirt and vest off and was stripped to the waist.

He looked like a Greek god, with steam rising from his rippling muscles, quickly freezing to form a cloud like a mystical mist around him.

The children always cheered MacLeod as the bus passed by - he was their hero!

I often wondered what inspired him to perform these Herculean tasks so, one day when he had just shovelled a trafficway through a deep snowdrift between Borenich and Croft Douglas, I invited MacLeod in to share a meal of mince and tatties with us, and then asked him.

After confessing that mince and tatties was his favourite food MacLeod went on, in lowered tones, to tell me how, one night at the fairground in Pitlochry, after the Highland games, he had felt compelled to enter a little tent with a sign outside saying, "Polly, the Premier Palmist in the World."

"So", he continued, "I went straight in before my nerve left me. But I needn't have worried.

"There was no hocus-pocus, crystal ball, dim lighting or crossing the palm with silver. Just two chairs with a really nice lady sitting on one of them.

"With a welcoming wave she invited me to be seated on the other one.

"Then she took hold of me by the hand with a grip that seemed to give me electrical shocks. She turned it over and gazed into my palm.

"But not for long. Her mind was quickly made up as she spoke slowly, so that her every word has stayed for ever with me.

"Some day, not so far away," she said, "a snow-white Arab

stallion will come prancing to you, with its silken mane and tail flying in the wind. It's then you must mount and ride with the wind in your hair, to a new life full of wonderment, just waiting for you!"

"That," said Peregrine with feeling, "is the one thing I think about every day. That's what drives me on."

It was my birthday the other day, and just as soon as the light flooded over the sky, I opened the front door and listened for the first birdsong.

It's a sort of special present delivered on this day every year and, even though there's a bitter, biting wind blowing off the snow-capped peaks, I am not disappointed.

There's a mistle thrush sitting on the swaying top of a silver spruce with snowflakes covering its bonny, spotted breast. He isn't called the Storm Cock for nothing.

His brave, sweet song is full of hope for the future with a message, not only for Aquarians, but everyone who thrills to the sheer magical music in the song of a bird.

Someone To Watch Over Me

For one devoted man, sleepless nights are spent on a stakeout, while a lonesome youngster brings fond memories flooding back for Gideon...

During lambing time a month or so ago, our local shepherd had almost forgotten what his bed looked like, because for four or five weeks he had to keep an almost continual, round-the-clock vigil over his flock, giving expert help when it was needed by ewes having a bit of bother.

It was sometimes necessary to create a sheltered spot for the newly-born lambs with bales of straw when a biting north-east wind blew with snowflakes on its breath, or the weather turned cold and wet.

It was also vital to provide protection against predators, particularly the foxes who creep down from their hiding places in the forests, and the "hoodie" crows perching on the tops of the tallest trees, continually watching for the slightest sign of weakness in any creature, large or small.

The shepherd knew to keep a watchful eye on the carrion or hooded crows, whose every movement could indicate where help might be urgently needed.

He also knew that the installation of powerful rays of flashing light, together with the repetitive bangs of automatic gas guns, have done little to deter the foxes.

They are highly intelligent, with keen minds which quickly come to the conclusion that, despite all this frightening display, there is no real danger here.

It's then that the foxes slip down in ones, twos, threes or even fours, from their watching places high upon the hilltops, to search furtively through the flocks of sheep hoping to find a helpless animal, like a ewe who has already had a lamb and is now busy giving birth to another.

That is the moment when the first-born, lying out on its own, can be in real danger.

Modern medical equipment, in the hands of veterinary surgeons, seems to help greatly in solving this problem, by giving a shepherd the opportunity to have his sheep scanned before giving birth.

This will tell which ewes are carrying twins so they can be taken from the rest of the flock to a safer pasture surrounded by wire netting and near the farm buildings, where a cry for help would always be answered, especially by the sheepdogs in the outside kennels.

Their super-sensitive noses soon sniff the smell of an approaching fox and that sets them barking furiously.

Foxes don't like domesticated dogs, especially working collies who are even more intelligent than they are, besides being bigger, stronger and just as agile.

Foxes are also aware that the sheepdogs will fight to the death, if necessary, to defend their flocks, but are invariably clever enough to avoid any such encounter.

There are those who say that, because some sheep have become so domesticated through the years, the ewes don't put up the same spirited defence against a predator that they used to, when quite a bit wilder.

If you doubt this, you only have to see the pure-bred black-faced ewe, well used to a lonely life on the hill, defending her lamb at the approach of what she thinks might be a menace to her little one.

With brown eyes blazing, she will fiercely stand guard over her baby.

Anyone or anything who does not heed the warning of her stamping forefeet faces the full charge of a "Hill Blackie" using her horned head as a battering ram, and that's a never-to-be-forgotten experience for man or beast!

Little lambs tend to grow up fast and quickly learn from their mothers to graze the short, sweet grass to supplement their milk supply.

Like children, the lambs gather together in groups. The boys continually challenge each other by wrestling, boxing and running races, whilst the girls have gentler games like "Queen of the Castle" on a little hillock and "Ring-A-Roses" around it, or hide-and-seek in the golden broom bushes.

In the field that we can see clearly from our kitchen window, there's a sturdy young lamb continuously calling for its mother who seems to have disappeared completely, with only a tell-tale track of wool leading to the lochside woods.

But the lamb is a resourceful little creature and has started circling around the flock trying to find a kindly ewe with some milk to spare.

So far, the little orphan hasn't had much luck in its search for a foster mother, being rebuffed by many who are obviously of the opinion that they already have plenty to cope with in the way of family commitments.

However, by the evening, the little wanderer, with its tail wagging twenty to the dozen, is sucking at the side of a friendly ewe who has more milk than her single baby can sup, and feels sorry for this lamb that has no mother.

The lonely lamb reminds me of when I left home, in my early teens, to work in Wigtownshire.

It took me a whole day to reach my destination, with plenty of time to think about how I would have to work a whole year away from home before being entitled to a week's holiday.

I felt so miserable on my arrival I could have caught the first train back, but didn't have the fare.

Fortunately, I met the Head Gamekeeper's wife - or, rather, she met me, with a warm embrace that even smelled like my mother!

The Head's wife obviously didn't believe in the saying that blood is thicker than water, and always gave me the same amount of love and affection that she afforded to her only son.

If I failed to show this lovely lady my full appreciation it was because I found it difficult to express my feelings at the time.

But I am sure she sensed this and, in any case, will know now that I thought the world of her.

Pride Of The Highlands

While Gideon takes an invigorating shower, some winter visitors are reaping the reward of their long, hard journey to the Strath...

Our supply of cool, clear water comes from several springs that trickle down from the mountain tops in the direction of Croft Douglas and, at various meeting points, merge together and race downhill in full flow.

The Highland spring is a law unto itself as to which direction it takes and often, because of rough terrain or some other reason, it may suddenly disappear underground.

Then the spring gains in strength and boils, grumbles and rumbles far below. The sound gets nearer and louder until the water surfaces with a roar that can be quite frightening, especially if you hear it after dark.

Our spring has now grown up into a gurgling, chuckling stream that flows down the east side of the house.

But first it fills the wishing well right to the top, then overflows to race along a bed of pebbles before plunging down in a waterfall, like a grey mare's silvery tail, onto a large flat stone that it has polished smooth through the years.

Douglas, who built our sturdy stone house, and his family all bathed under this sparkling waterfall and, although the water is now piped into the house, I still sometimes sneak out in the early morning and sample a shower under the "grey mare's tail."

It's an enchanting experience and also a chance to see another "dipper", the water ouzel.

It's like a blackbird with a short tail and without a yellow bill.

But it does wear a big, spotted, white bib on its breast and has a body that is wedge-shaped and specially designed for upstream underwater work.

How diligently the dipper searches the bed of the burn, turning over all the small stones and pebbles, looking for tasty bites.

I could have watched for a lot longer, but it gets a bit chilly standing under our outdoor shower.

We are so proud of our Highland spring water, and summer visitors from all over the world marvel at its cool, clear purity.

One French couple sipped and said, "Magnifique!" and enquired as to the charge.

I explained that water, here in a Highland croft, was free.

They then chorused together, "Mon ami, in France we pay for pond water!"

So it came as a bit of a shock when recently, a young man brandishing a card bearing his photograph and proclaiming he was an official of some sort, appeared on our doorstep.

He informed us that, under European Community rules, all private water supplies had to be checked.

I thought this was an intrusion on people's liberty, which we place a high value on here, but he was such a pleasant young man that I decided there was no real harm in it and allowed him to take samples of our spring water.

Looking at one he held up, he said in what I hoped was mock alarm, "What is this?"

"This" was a tiny creature that wriggled up and down and around the cylindrical sample glass.

I hastened to explain as lightheartedly as I could that this was a baby water shrimp that had somehow squirmed and finally squeezed through the fine mesh filter that lies in the bed of the spring.

It keeps the water that flows into the tank supplying our house free from any "undesirables."

The official, although not of the stern-faced variety, didn't look sufficiently convinced by my explanation.

But he finally succumbed when I scooped up the escapee with a teaspoon and told him that this occasionally happened. When it did, we always returned the babies to the spring, because freshwater shrimps will not survive in anything but the purest water!

The fieldfares are here now in huge flocks.

They are thrushes from Scandinavia and very attractive birds, boldly marked with silver-grey feathers on their heads and backs.

Just like the wild geese from Greenland, they seem confident that our winter will be a whole lot better than in their homeland, and that food will be more plentiful.

The dark purple sloeberries and bunches of red rowans are in scarcer supply here this year, but Dame Nature is never caught out when it comes to setting the table for winter and always has a few secrets up her green sleeves - like the wild crab apple trees.

This spring their blossom was like a heavy fall of snow, and now the little apples, with their rosy cheeks, are everywhere. The first of the wintry winds has sent them plummeting down to form colourful circles around their parent trees.

The fieldfares are very fond of apples, tackling those that are still clinging to the treetops first, then flitting down to feed on the fallen fruit lying below, which they don't seem to mind sharing with the fieldmice and red squirrels.

But the fieldfares have saved something special to savour after consuming the crab apples.

After fully five years of waiting, our wild plum trees seemingly decided that this was the time to bear fruit and, when a wild plum tree makes up its mind, it doesn't mean maybe!

All around them the ground is covered with a carpet of delicious, deep purple plums, with some fruit still clinging determinedly to the tops.

This fantastic feast will certainly give the fieldfares something to talk about when they go back home.

Irralee sometimes likes to sit by our waterfall. She worries, though, what the official, tentatively carrying out EC orders, would have said had he seen the little trout circling at the bottom of the well, showing off its silvery sides spotted with brilliant red and blue, then suddenly shooting up to the surface with a flirt of its tail.

Drumbuie makes the final decision about our Highland spring water by having a long, satisfying sup before settling down for the night.

A Fine Romance

While the first rays of the summer sun fill the Croft Douglas "lodgers" with get-up-and-go, Gideon recalls how one lonely man was at a loss when love was in the air...

For as long as I can remember, we haven't had a chance to redecorate the Croft Douglas stairway ceiling because of all the butterflies who flock through the purposefully left-open porch door, and colourfully cover the ceiling at the top of the stairs for at least seven months of the year.

I wonder if this is because it was last painted a light primrose yellow in an attempt to lighten up a somewhat dark stairway with a little artificial sunshine.

Or perhaps it's because this place has a more even temperature than anywhere else in the house, being neither too hot nor too cold.

Only the beautiful tortoiseshell butterflies seem to know.

It's a source of amazement to me how these lovely, delicately designed fragments of life survive all summer, flitting from flower to flower, sipping nectar and storing up enough of this sugary sweetness to allow them to sleep for around seven months.

Then they're awakened by the warmth of yet another summer to do their carefree sunshine dancing all over again.

For weeks now, the butterflies have been restlessly sleepwalking around the staircase walls, slowly being roused by the tender touch of searching sunbeams.

Some even venture downstairs, singly or in twos and threes, to flutter excitedly against the large panes of glass in the porch that so tantalisingly give them a view of the paradise outside.

It's then we always make a point of carefully closing the porch door, in case our beautiful butterflies are tempted to "take off" just when the weather could take a turn for the worse.

Choosing the right time to let them go is a responsibility that weighs much more than a butterfly, as fragile as a flake of snow.

Uilleam was a hard worker in his croft high up in the hills. The only way to wrest a living from his hill land was to take part in the business of buying and selling.

To prevent this becoming a dull, dismal affair, he loved to liven things up a bit. As he so perfectly put it, "Ye hae to hae a haggle!"

The haggling process began with a long, drawn-out discussion about whatever he was buying or selling, with occasional intervals for silent thinking.

This usually resulted in a series of sighs and simulated worry about parting with something at a "giveaway" price, followed by much headshaking, until he finally slapped the buyer's or seller's hand to seal the deal.

This was a sure sign that the haggle was over and both had made a bargain that neither would ever go back on.

One day, Uilleam's wife took a dizzy turn and, as he himself put it, "just slipped away," leaving Uilleam to bring up their teenage daughter, Flora, on his own.

She was formed in the same mould as her mother, inheriting the finely chiselled features, even temperament, competent, easy-going approach to life and last but not least, her great culinary skills.

So Flora took over where her mum had left off, looking after her father by blithely Highland dancing through the housework and singing the songs her mother had sung whilst preparing a mouth-watering meal.

What's more, she was ready to be called on to give her dad a hand with the animals, too.

Uilleam was a man of few words but never, ever slow to show his appreciation.

Every market day, no matter if the trading had been good, bad or indifferent, Uilleam went out of his way to get some suitable present for Flora, sometimes bringing home a box of her favourite dark chocolates with soft centres because she had also inherited her mother's sweet tooth!

Uilleam knew, too, that elaborate make-up wasn't in Flora's line but a subtle perfume was something she just couldn't resist.

Flora had many admirers among the young men from the glens, but they mostly feared her father's stern, critical gaze and fled.

All except Duncan.

He was the son of a cattle rancher in the West who had been sent to the Strath at lambing time to learn something about sheep.

Duncan soon found favour with Uilleam by giving him some expert help which made what could have been difficult calving for his favourite milk cow an easy affair.

So Uilleam was glad to lend Duncan his pony when he wanted to make a short cut through the hills to look at a 500 acre farm that was on the market for a modest rental.

But before he left, Duncan confided to Flora that if and when the farm was his, he would have no hesitation in seeking her hand in marriage.

Flora was so excited she told her father, but Uilleam wasn't at all happy about the possibility of losing his devoted daughter and so he was relieved when Duncan came back, shaking his head and saying the farm wasn't good enough.

Although Uilleam commiserated with the young couple, he was secretly delighted, until he saw the tears glistening in Flora's eyes.

So, drawing Duncan aside, he asked, "What was wrong with the place?"

Duncan answered in disappointed tones, "The land was a mass of bunches of bright yellow flowers standing on long, strong stems."

"Aha", exclaimed Uilleam, "that would be ragwort. It can be poisonous to horses and cattle at a certain time of year.

"We always called it `Stinking Willie' because of the strong smell from its flowers."

"That's them," agreed Duncan. "They were two or three feet tall. In fact, I tethered your pony to one of them."

"You did what?" gasped Uilleam, jumping up from his seat. "You must ride back and claim that place. I will tell you how to get rid of the ragwort."

Whilst they were saddling the pony, Uilleam explained that ragwort could only grow so strong in soil that was really rich.

Flora was over the moon when Duncan told her that he had taken on the farm thanks to her father's advice.

Uilleam was as good as his word and told Duncan that ragwort doesn't seem to harm sheep, adding with a wink, "That's why I'm giving you a wedding present of forty blackface sheep."

The farm proved to be as rich as Uilleam had predicted and it wasn't long before his unselfishness was rewarded by the sight of Flora sitting up in bed, cradling his first grandchild.

He tried so hard to say something, but just couldn't get the words out.

So they both settled for a big hug and a kiss while Flora whispered, "Don't worry, Dad, you won't ever be left alone. Remember, a daughter's a daughter all her life."